Best Hikes Near
Houston

D1462443

Best Hikes Near
Houston

KEITH STELTER

FALCONGUIDES

GUILFORD, CONNECTICUT
HELENA, MONTANA

AN IMPRINT OF GLOBE PEQUOT PRESS

FALCONGUIDES®

Copyright © 2011 by Morris Book Publishing, LLC

ALL RIGHTS RESERVED. No part of this book may be reproduced or transmitted in any form by any means, electronic or mechanical, including photocopying and recording, or by any information storage and retrieval system, except as may be expressly permitted in writing from the publisher. Requests for permission should be addressed to Globe Pequot Press, Attn: Rights and Permissions Department, P.O. Box 480, Guilford, CT 06437.

FalconGuides is an imprint of Globe Pequot Press.
Falcon, FalconGuides, and Outfit Your Mind are registered trademarks of Morris Book Publishing, LLC.

Interior photos: Keith Stelter, except page 191, which is courtesy of Harris County, Pct3, Kleb Woods Nature Preserve Collection
Art on page iii © Shutterstock

Text design: Sheryl P. Kober
Layout: Maggie Peterson
Project editor: Julie Marsh
Maps: Trailhead Graphics, Inc. © Morris Book Publishing, LLC

Library of Congress Cataloging-in-Publication data is available on file.
ISBN 978-0-7627-5951-4

Printed in China
10 9 8 7 6 5 4 3 2 1

Contents

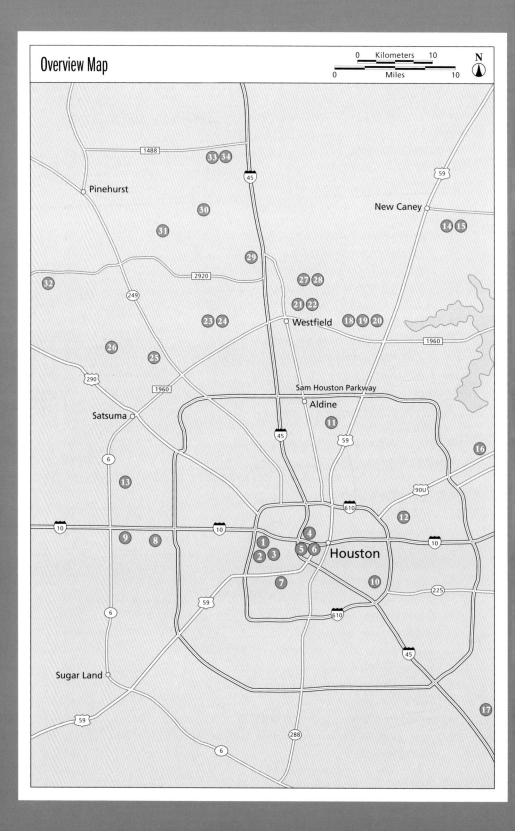

Overview Map

0　Kilometers　10

0　Miles　10

N

Pinehurst

New Caney

1488

33 34

45

30

31

59

14 15

32

249

2920

29

27 28

21 22

23 24

26

25

Westfield

18 19 20

1960

290

1960

Sam Houston Parkway

Satsuma

45

Aldine

11

59

16

6

13

90U

10

10

9　8

12

10

1

2　3

4

5　6

Houston

7

10

225

610

6

59

610

Sugar Land

45

59

17

288

6

Acknowledgments

Many people helped make this book possible, and a few went "beyond the call of duty." Thanks to Mark, Scott, and Kay Stelter for their encouragement, ideas, patience, and proofreading, and to Kim Stelter and Nate Enloe for hiking and journaling with me. And thanks to park superintendent Roy Vasquez for his help on Herman Brown Park, Mike Howlett for his help on Jesse Jones Park, Bobby J. Martin and Sandy Poché at Pundt Park, and Terri MacArthur with Legacy Land Trust. Dozens of other people provided information about history, geology, flora and fauna, and hikes they considered "the best hikes near Houston." I appreciate their work and thank all of them.

Many hikers add a dimension to their hike by taking pictures.

Introduction

Whether providing recreational or educational opportunities, encouraging well-being, exploring history and geology, or bringing together people of all ages, hiking has become an important part of many people's lives. The purpose of this guide is to introduce readers to the variety of hiking opportunities in the Houston area. In many hiking guides the hike descriptions are generally point-to-point narratives, getting you safely from the trailhead to the trail's end and back again. However, including information on area flora, fauna, history, and geology adds a great deal of interest to many hikers, including families with young children.

I spent several months researching, talking with park personnel and other folks, hiking and sometimes rehiking trails, and studying the area for interesting facts, scenery, history, geology, and potential photographs. I talked with a variety of hikers, asking them what they wanted a hike description to cover and what made a "best hike near Houston." I used the following criteria to select the hikes included in this guide: fun, exercise, family experience, scenery, history, bayous, first-time hiker, experienced hiker, moderate length (1 to 5 miles), dog friendliness, and wheelchair accessibility. Loops and interconnecting loop trails were selected

Acres of bluebonnets, the state flower of Texas, line the highways during spring.

where possible so that a "best" hike within a park could be fashioned by combining the best of several trails.

Determining the best hikes near Houston was a combination of personal judgment about the level of hiker the hike was geared toward and information from park staff and other hikers. Four of my favorite hikes are the varied trails at Jesse Jones Park, the interconnecting loops in Memorial Park, the Bear Creek Trail, and the Herman Brown Park trails. Hiking city and county trails offers a different experience from hiking in state parks and on backcountry trails.

> **Hiking city and county trails offers a different experience from hiking in state parks and on backcountry trails.**

Most of the city trails are multipurpose and paved, and a few are lighted at night, creating an entirely new hiking experience. There can also be the distraction of the city itself, with its busy streets, buildings, and commerce, but a surprisingly good number of the trails are in wooded areas, providing an unexpected degree of solitude.

The photographs included in this guide were chosen to whet your curiosity about a hike. The sidebars and tips are meant to be enjoyable and educational, helping to make this a family book. I hope that at least some of the hikes in this

Red-eared turtles sun themselves in the middle of a cypress swamp. Notice the knobby knees on the bald cypress trees.

guide will become your personal favorites and that this book will prove an informative and interesting read as well as an excellent guide to the best hikes near Houston.

Hiking in Houston

Bayous are shallow, slow-moving creeks or minor rivers found in low-lying southern states, and with four major bayous passing through it, Houston is justifiably called the "Bayou City." Buffalo Bayou runs into downtown, Brays Bayou passes near the Texas Medical Center, White Oak Bayou flows through the Heights, and Sims Bayou lies in the south of Houston. Originally the bayous were used exclusively for flood control, but since the city recognized the opportunity to build trails along them, they have become a bonanza for hikers.

Due to the efforts of Terese "Terry" Hershey; her husband, Jacob; young congressman George H. W. Bush; Texas businessman George Mitchell; and a dedicated group of supporters, Buffalo Bayou was saved from having its sides lined with concrete in the 1960s and 1970s. Because of this, the bayou contains an incredibly diverse ecosystem that supports dozens of species of flora and fauna, which add an extra dimension to your hike. Buffalo Bayou winds its way through dozens of suburban communities, giving you the opportunity to find a trail near your neighborhood. From West Houston the bayou heads toward downtown. After passing Barker Reservoir, it runs through Terry Hershey Park (Hike 9) to the Houston Arboretum (Hikes 2 and 3), then to Memorial Park (Hike 1) and through downtown Houston (Hikes 4, 5, and 6). White Oak and Buffalo Bayous join in downtown Houston at an area known as Allen's Landing. This is the point where the Allen brothers landed in 1836 and founded Houston.

Hiking in Houston is more than walking along bayous, though. Trails can be found in woods and nature sanctuaries, along community streets, downtown, or on a 1-square-block oasis in the middle of a residential community. Some trails are busy with hikers, joggers, and cyclists; others are secluded and far from downtown.

The opportunity to vary the scenery you pass on a hike is almost unlimited. The Central and Coastal Flyways pass over or near the city, affording a year-round opportunity to enjoy an array of native and migratory birds that use the bayous for shelter and food. Birds to look for throughout the year include ospreys, cardinals, herons, hawks, and egrets. More than 300 of the 600 bird species recorded in the state have been seen in this region.

The best indication of birds being present is hearing their songs. The bluebird sings *chur-lee chur chur-lee,* the eastern phoebe repeats *fee-bee fee-bee* from the tops of branches, and the tufted titmouse makes a loud whistlelike *peter-peter-peter.* Some of the area's most colorful birds include the red-breasted nuthatch, eastern bluebird, yellow-throated warbler, dickcissel, pileated woodpecker, American goldfinch, vermilion flycatcher, hooded merganser, and numerous other ducks.

Most mammals are active during the night, so seeing them can be difficult. Look for their tracks around the trail and near streams or bayous. White-tailed deer, nine-banded armadillos (the state small mammal), coyotes, opossums, foxes, raccoons, skunks, and fox squirrels make their homes here. Squirrels, white-tailed deer, and armadillos are especially common in many hiking areas.

In the spring and early summer, when wildflowers set the roadsides ablaze with color, driving to a hiking location can be a visual feast. Commonly seen are yellow coreopsis, red firewheels, phlox, Mexican hats, daisies, purple winecups, and yellow primroses. The Texas bluebonnet, the state flower, is at its peak in late March and early April.

The Texas Parks & Wildlife Department has developed a series of nature trails, including the Great Texas Birding Trail–Central Coast and the Heart of Texas Wildlife Trail–East. Maps and location markers at the sites reference areas where wildlife may be seen.

A male white egret brings nesting materials to his mate. Nests are constructed in the spring.

Houston is the largest city in Texas and the fourth largest in the United States, and its land area is also very big. This is an advantage to hikers, since much of the city was built on forested land, marshes, swamps, or prairie. Some of these areas have been set aside as parks, with miles of trails. The trails along the bayous are called "linear" because they follow the bayou and are generally out-and-back hikes.

The Energy Corridor District was recently selected by the National Park Service's Rivers, Trails and Conservation Assistance Program to receive planning assistance for the West Houston Trail System. Through this partnership, the Park Service and Energy Corridor District will continue to develop and improve trails throughout the area. This is great for hikers and will create opportunities not found anywhere else in the country.

The Houston Parks and Recreation Department's trail system spans more than 102 miles. The Harris County Precinct Parks Department trails cover more than 80 miles.

Enjoy the experience of hiking in eastern Texas. The great ecological diversity of the territory, along with the flora and fauna, allows you to fashion trips that are much more than just "hikes in the woods." City hiking trails are sometimes sidewalks, and some have been widened from the conventional 4-foot sidewalk to as much as 8 feet to allow multiuse. Some of these "trails" have been designed as "traffic lanes" to accommodate people walking and biking to work as well as recreationists.

Cypress swamps are common to several Houston trails. The bald cypress tree is easy to identify due to its knobby roots extending out of the water.

Houston Weather

Houston's climate is subtropical with high humidity. Mild winds from the south and southeast carry heat from deserts in Mexico and bring rain, sometimes very heavy, from the Gulf of Mexico. The average low temperature (41 degrees Fahrenheit) is in January, and the average high (94 degrees) is in July and August. The average yearly rainfall is 47.9 inches. The wettest month is June, averaging 5.3 inches, followed closely by May's 5.2 inches. The driest month is February, with 3 inches of rain. Current weather and forecasts for the Houston area can be obtained by calling the park contact for the hike you are considering. Except for high temperatures and humidity in July and August and possible showers in May, the weather for hiking in the area is great.

Average Monthly Temperatures

Month	High	Low
Jan	62	41
Feb	67	44
Mar	73	51
Apr	79	58
May	86	66
June	91	72
July	94	74
Aug	94	73
Scpt	89	68
Oct	82	59
Nov	72	50
Dec	65	43

Average Precipitation (Rainfall)

Month	Inches
Jan	3.7
Feb	3.0
Mar	3.4
Apr	3.6
May	5.2
June	5.3
July	3.2
Aug	3.8
Sept	4.3
Oct	4.5
Nov	4.2
Dec	3.7

Zero Impact and Trail Etiquette

We have a responsibility to protect, no longer just conquer and use, our wild places. Many public hiking locations are at risk, so please do what you can to use them wisely. The following points will help you better understand what it means to take care of parks and wild places while still making the most of your hiking experience.

- Stay on the trail. Anyone can take a hike, but hiking safely and with good conservation practices is an art requiring preparation and proper equipment. Always leave an area as good as—or preferably better—than you found it. Key to doing this is staying on the trail.

  It's true that a trail anywhere leads nowhere new, but purists will just have to get over it. Trails serve an important purpose: They limit impact on natural areas. Straying from a designated trail can cause damage to sensitive areas— damage that may take the area years to recover from, if it can recover at all. Even simple shortcuts can be destructive.

  Many of the hikes described in this guide are on or near areas ecologically important to supporting endangered flora and fauna. So please, stay on the trail.

- Leave no weeds. Noxious weeds tend to overtake other plants, which in turn affects animals and birds that depend on native plants for food. To minimize the spread of noxious weeds, regularly clean your boots and hiking poles of

A large Ilo moth on a leaf. Notice the fake eyes on its wings.

mud and seeds and brush your dog to remove any weed seeds before heading into a new area. Non-native invasive plants such as yaupon are particularly destructive and can quickly destroy acres of habitat.

- Keep your dog under control. Always obey leash laws, and be sure to bury your dog's waste or pack it out in resealable plastic bags.
- Respect other trail users. Often you won't be the only one on the trail. With the rise in popularity of multiuse trails, you'll have to learn a new kind of respect, beyond the nod and "hello" approach of the past. First investigate whether you're on a multiuse trail, and then assume the appropriate precautions. Mountain bikers can be like stealth airplanes—you may not hear them coming. Be prepared and find out ahead of time whether you'll be sharing the trail with them. Cyclists should always yield to hikers, but that's little comfort to the hiker who gets overrun. Be aware, and stay to the right. More trails are being designed to be, at least in part, wheelchair accessible. Always step to the side to allow folks in wheelchairs time to navigate the terrain. Make them aware if you are going to pass around them.

First Aid

Sunburn

Wear sunscreen or sunblock, protective clothing, and a wide-brimmed hat. If you do get sunburn, protect the affected area from further sun exposure and treat it with aloe vera gel or a treatment of your choice. Remember that your eyes are vulnerable to damaging radiation as well. Sunglasses can help prevent eye damage from the sun.

Blisters

Be prepared to take care of these hike spoilers by carrying moleskin (a lightly padded adhesive) or gauze and tape. An effective way to apply moleskin is to cut out a circle of the material, remove the center—like a doughnut—and place it over the blistered area.

Insect Bites and Stings

You can treat most insect bites and stings by taking an anti-inflammatory pain medication and using ice to reduce swelling. A cold compress can sometimes ease the itching and discomfort. Don't pinch or scratch the area—you'll only spread the venom.

Ticks

Ticks can carry diseases such as Rocky Mountain spotted fever and Lyme disease. The best defense is, of course, prevention. If you know you're going to be hiking through an area containing ticks, wear long pants and a long-sleeved shirt. At the end of your hike, do a spot check for ticks (and insects in general).

Poison Ivy, Oak, and Sumac

These skin irritants are prevalent on many of the trails in east Texas, sometimes growing into the trail. They come in the form of a bush or a vine and have leaflets in groups of three (poison ivy and oak), five, seven, or nine. Learn how to spot the plants, and especially show young children what to look for. Few things can spoil a hike, or your life the week after, more than coming into contact with poison ivy, oak, or sumac. The allergic reaction, in the form of blisters, usually develops about 12 hours after exposure.

The best defense against these irritants is to wear clothing that covers your arms, legs, and torso. If you think you came into contact with these plants, wash the affected area with soap and water as soon as possible. If the rash spreads, you may need to see a doctor.

A Texas forest ranger on the left and a representative from the Legacy Land Trust stand beside a record-setting bald cypress tree. Record-size specimans are recorded and protected.

How to Use This Guide

Thirty-four hikes are detailed in this guide. The overview map at the beginning of the book shows the location of each hike by number, keyed to the table of contents. Each hike is accompanied by a route map that shows access roads, the highlighted featured route, and directional arrows to point you in the right direction. It indicates the general outline of the hike. Due to scale restrictions, it is not as detailed as a park map might be or even as our Miles and Directions are. While most of the hikes are on clearly designated paths, use these route maps in conjunction with other resources.

To aid in quick decision making, each hike description begins with a short summary to give you a taste of the hiking adventure to follow. You'll learn about the trail terrain and what surprises the route has to offer. Next you'll find the quick, nitty-gritty details of the hike: hike distance and type (loop, lollipop, or out and back); approximate hiking time; difficulty rating; type of trail surface; best season for the hike; other trail users; canine compatibility; fees and permits; park schedule; map resources; trail contacts; and additional information that will help you on your trek.

Finding the trailhead provides directions from Houston right down to where you'll want to park your car. **The Hike** is the meat of the chapter. Detailed and honest, it's a carefully researched impression of the trail. While it's impossible to cover everything, you can rest assured that you won't miss what's important. **Miles and Directions** provides mileage cues that identify all turns and trail name changes, as well as points of interest.

Don't feel restricted to the routes and trails mapped in this guide. Stick to marked trails, but be adventurous and use the book as a platform to discover new routes for yourself. One of the simplest ways to begin is to turn the map upside down and hike the trail in reverse. The change in perspective can make the hike feel quite different—it's like getting two hikes for one.

You will find **Green Tips** scattered throughout the guide. These are offered as suggestions for ways to reduce your impact both on the trails and on the planet.

You may wish to copy the directions for the course onto a small sheet of paper to help you while hiking, or photocopy the map and cue sheet to take with you. Otherwise, just slip the whole book in your pocket and take it with you. Enjoy your time in the outdoors—and remember to pack out what you pack in.

Trail Finder

Hike No.	Hike Name	Best Hikes for Families and Children	Best Hikes for Bayou/Stream Lovers	Best Hikes for History Lovers	Best Hikes for Nature Lovers and Bird-Watchers	Best Hikes for Dogs	Best Hikes for the Physically Challenged	Best Hikes for Runners	Best Hikes for Sun Lovers	Best Hikes for Forest Lovers
1	Memorial Park: Purple, Orange, Yellow, Red, and Blue Trails			●	●	●				
2	Houston Arboretum: Outer Loop	●			●	●				
3	Houston Arboretum: Inner Loop	●			●	●				
4	Buffalo Bayou: Tinsley Trail	●	●			●	●	●	●	
5	Buffalo Bayou: Blue Lagoon Trail	●	●	●		●	●			
6	Buffalo Bayou: Sabine to Waugh		●				●	●	●	
7	Hermann Park	●		●			●	●		
8	Edith L. Moore Nature Sanctuary	●	●		●		●			●
9	Terry Hershey Park: Cardinal and Blue Jay Trails					●		●	●	
10	John T. Mason Park	●	●			●	●	●	●	
11	Keith-Weiss Park	●	●		●		●		●	
12	Herman Brown Park				●	●				●
13	Bear Creek Nature Trail				●					●
14	Lake Houston Wilderness Park: Hoot Owl and Magnolia Trails	●			●					●

Trail Finder

Hike No.	Hike Name	Best Hikes for Families and Children	Best Hikes for Bayou/Stream Lovers	Best Hikes for History Lovers	Best Hikes for Nature Lovers and Bird-Watchers	Best Hikes for Dogs	Best Hikes for the Physically Challenged	Best Hikes for Runners	Best Hikes for Sun Lovers	Best Hikes for Forest Lovers
15	Lake Houston Wilderness Park: Peach Creek Loop and Forest Trail		●		●					●
16	Sheldon Lake State Park: Pond Loop, Bent Pine, and Swamp Rabbit Trails	●	●							
17	Armand Bayou Nature Center: Karankawa Trail and Prairie Platform	●	●							●
18	Jesse Jones Park: Judy Overby Bell Trail						●			●
19	Jesse Jones Park: Palmetto, Cypress, High Bank, and White Oak Trails	●			●					
20	Jesse Jones Park: Canoe, Cypress Overlook, River Birch, and Spring Creek Trails		●		●					
21	Mercer Arboretum: East Oxbow and Little and Big Cypress Loops	●					●			
22	Mercer Arboretum: Cypress Pond, Hickory Bog, Oxbow, and Big Thicket Loops	●								●
23	Collins Park: Gourley Nature Trail							●	●	

Trail Finder

Hike No.	Hike Name	Best Hikes for Families and Children	Best Hikes for Bayou/Stream Lovers	Best Hikes for History Lovers	Best Hikes for Nature Lovers and Bird-Watchers	Best Hikes for Dogs	Best Hikes for the Physically Challenged	Best Hikes for Runners	Best Hikes for Sun Lovers	Best Hikes for Forest Lovers
24	Collins Park: Cypress Creek Greenway		●		●			●		
25	Faulkey Gully Trail						●	●	●	
26	Little Cypress Creek Preserve: Pond Loop Trail		●		●					
27	Pundt Park: Pundt Lake, Creekside, Walnut, Red Bay, and Hardwood Trails					●				
28	Pundt Park: Spring Creek Greenway and Fallen Pine Trail									●
29	Montgomery County Preserve: Loop Trail, Creek Loop, and Pond Loop	●	●		●					●
30	George Mitchell Preserve: Nature Loop Trail									●
31	Burroughs Park: Nature and Lake Trails	●								●
32	Kleb Woods Nature Preserve: Farm, Wetlands, and Nature Center Trails			●	●					
33	Jones Forest: Sweetleaf Nature Trail	●			●					
34	Jones Forest: Middle Lake Hiking Trail									●

Map Legend

Transportation

- **10** Freeway/Interstate Highway
- **59** U.S. Highway
- **6** State Highway
- **1488** Other Road
- = = = = Unpaved Road
- Railroad

Trails

- Selected Route
- Trail
- → Direction of Route

Water Features

- Body of Water
- River or Creek
- Intermittent River
- Swamp

Symbols

- **20** Trailhead
- ■ Building/Point of Interest
- Park Office
- **P** Parking
- Restroom
- Scenic View
- **?** Visitor Center
- Drinking Water
- Picnic Area
- **A** Campground
- Bridge
- Gate
- Boardwalk
- ○ Towns and Cities

Land Management

- Local Park

Memorial Park: Purple, Orange, Yellow, Red, and Blue Trails

Combine portions of the Purple, Orange, Yellow, Red, and Blue Trails into a loop that covers the most interesting areas of Memorial Park—the largest urban park in Texas, nearly double the size of New York's Central Park. Camp Logan, a World War I army training camp, occupied this site from 1917 to 1923. The family of James Hogg (governor of Texas from 1891 to 1895) sold 1,503 acres to the city in 1924 and later donated another 1,000 acres for the park.

Start: Purple Trail trailhead adjacent to parking area on North Picnic Lane

Distance: 2.4-mile loop

Approximate hiking time: 1.75 hours

Difficulty: Moderate due to winding narrow trails with some elevation changes

Trail surface: Crushed granite, dirt

Seasons: Year-round

Other trail users: Dog walkers, mountain bikers

Canine compatibility: Leashed dogs permitted

Fees and permits: None required

Schedule: 6 a.m.–11 p.m.

Maps: None available in the park. Maps are available at www.memorialparkconservancy.org. USGS: Houston Heights.

Trail contact: Houston Parks and Recreation Department (HPARD), 2999 South Wayside Dr., Houston 77023; (713) 865-4500; www.houstontx.gov/parks/trails.html

Other: There is a portable toilet by the parking area and a hose for water. No potable water or restrooms on the trail.

Finding the trailhead: From the intersection of I-10 and Loop I-610, take Loop I-610 South to Memorial Drive exit 10. Head east on Memorial Drive into the park and follow Memorial Drive to North Picnic Lane; turn right. Take an immediate right to the ball field parking lot. *DeLorme: Texas Atlas & Gazetteer:* Page 129, I11. GPS: N29 45.883' / W95 26.488'

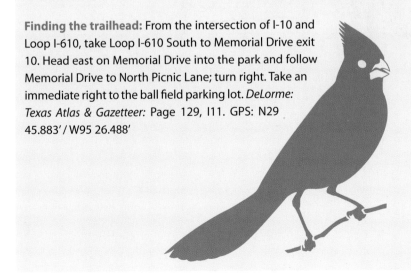

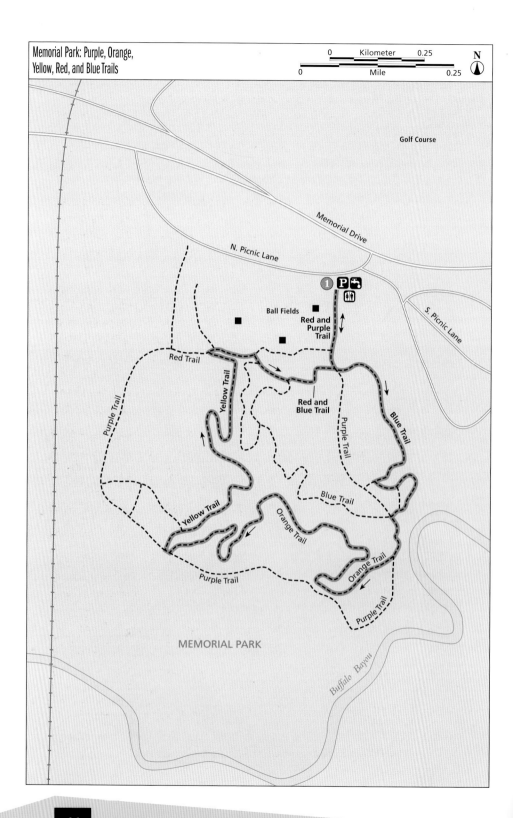

Memorial Park: Purple, Orange, Yellow, Red, and Blue Trails

Golf Course

Memorial Drive

N. Picnic Lane

S. Picnic Lane

Ball Fields

Red and Purple Trail

Red Trail

Yellow Trail

Purple Trail

Red and Blue Trail

Purple Trail

Blue Trail

Yellow Trail

Blue Trail

Orange Trail

Purple Trail

Orange Trail

Purple Trail

MEMORIAL PARK

Buffalo Bayou

THE HIKE

Start at the Purple Trail trailhead adjacent to the parking area on North Picnic Lane. Ball fields are on the right. This collection of trails is often referred to as the Ho Chi Minh Trail, possibly because it's heavily wooded, even jungle-like, but the paths are easy to follow and the atmosphere is cool and green. These are among the best trails inside the I-610 Loop in Houston. Depending on the season, mosquitoes can be annoying, so be prepared.

The trail quickly veers left at the trailhead, away from the ball fields, and passes a path on the right identified on a marker post as the Red Trail. Stay on the Purple Trail, going through heavy woods of live oaks, black cherry trees, and loblolly pines. The path is flat, with tangled tree roots crossing it. If just the Purple Trail were followed, it would form a large loop back to the trailhead.

Reach a Y and follow the Blue Trail to the left as it undulates up and down and is sometimes single-track. There are numerous gullies, some with drop-offs of 30 feet, at the trail's edge. Mountain bikers use all of these trails, so stay to the right and be alert. Opossums, squirrels, armadillos, raccoons, rabbits, coyotes, turtles, and snakes call this area home. Most likely only squirrels will be seen, but watching for tracks can be interesting.

Stay on the Blue Trail to an intersection with the Purple Trail. Head left (southeast) on the Purple Trail. Numerous species of birds can be seen throughout the

Three generations of hikers investigate items on the trail to record in their log book.

year. Watch for ruby-throated hummingbirds, especially in the fall. Proceed to an intersection on the right with the Orange Trail.

Head southwest then northeast on the Orange Trail. The right edge of the trail has drop-offs into ravines, while the left edge is flat. Pass by some very large lob-lolly pines—3 feet in diameter and 80 feet tall. Reach the T where the Orange Trail dead-ends into the Purple Trail. Turn right onto the Purple Trail. Depending on the season, swallowtails, painted ladies, and other butterflies may be seen.

Watch for the connector path to the Yellow Trail and follow it north. Go down a steep slope to a wooden bridge that crosses a seasonal creek bed. This section is also called the West Ridge Trail. There are some steep drop-offs, going down 25 feet, at the trail's edge. Some sections of the trail are single-track. Follow short sections of the Red, Blue, and Purple Trails until you reach the trailhead.

MILES AND DIRECTIONS

Note: All the trails have marker posts identifying them.

0.0 Start at the Purple Trail trailhead adjacent to the south end of the parking area off North Picnic Lane.

0.1 Pass a small path on the right (west) with the Red Trail marker post. Continue straight on the Purple Trail.

0.2 Reach a Y and take the left (east) branch, which is the Blue Trail. The Purple and Red/Blue Trails continue to the right.

0.3 Pass a Blue Trail marker post on the left. Continue following the Blue Trail in a generally southern direction.

0.4 Trail zigzags through the woods, sometimes bending hard left and then hard right.

0.5 Just before reaching the Purple Trail, turn left (east) with the Blue Trail. Trail marker posts identify the trails. In a couple hunderd feet, reach a chain-link fence blocking mountain bikers. A shortcut that can be dangerous goes right; bear slightly left to get around the fence and then continue straight on the Blue Trail.

0.7 Travel down a slope and then pass over a culvert. Reach a Y and take the right branch onto the Orange Trail, heading southwest. As the Orange Trail nears the Purple Trail again, turn sharply right, to the northeast, and continue following the Orange Trail.

1.1 Reach a T where the Orange Trail dead-ends into the Purple Trail. Turn right, following the right branch west. Continue following the Purple Trail. In a few hundred feet, the Purple Trail meets a connector path to the Yellow Trail to the right. Take the connector path, heading north to the Yellow Trail. Trail marker posts are at this junction.

1.2 Follow the connector path to where it Ts with the Yellow Trail. Take the right branch, heading northeast. This is also called the West Ridge Trail.

1.4 Pass a Yellow Trail marker post on the left. Continue following the Yellow Trail in a generally northern direction.

1.7 Pass a Yellow Trail marker post on the right. Continue following the Yellow Trail north.

1.9 Reach a junction where the Yellow Trail ends and meets the Purple Trail, with the Red Trail on the right. Turn hard right onto the Red Trail and immediately reach a Y. Take the right branch, heading east. The left branch is also the Red Trail.

2.0 Continue straight east, following the Red Trail. Pass an intersection on the left, which is also a section of the Red Trail.

2.1 Reach a T where the Red Trail dead-ends into the Blue Trail. Take the left branch, heading east on the Blue Trail.

2.3 Reach a junction where the Blue Trail crosses over the Purple Trail. Turn left (north) onto the Purple Trail and backtrack the short distance to the trailhead.

2.4 End the hike at the Purple Trail trailhead and return to the parking lot.

Spiders Aren't Scary

While visiting my daughter and her family, I went out on the porch with Samantha Jo (who everybody calls Sammy), my seven-year-old granddaughter. I saw a large spider web hanging from the corner of the porch ceiling. "Sammy," I said, "Why don't you have your dad brush that spider web away? Spiders are scary." I've had an arm's-length attitude toward spiders since I was a young boy and read that naturalist John Muir died from the bite of a brown recluse spider. Also, walking into their webs across a trail has never engendered any kind feelings.

Sammy quickly answered, "Spiders are not scary! Well, when my mommy and I first saw the spider, I was a little afraid. But now, Briana is my friend!"

Taken aback, I said, "You've named the spider? How do you know it's a she?" She replied, "Because my daddy saw it was having a baby and told me." I asked her what she did then. She told me that every day she and her dad or mom watched the spider.

"Daddy told me a lot of things about spiders." I asked if she knew what kind of spider it was. I was informed that the spider was an orb weaver. I suggested that maybe we should go back to the porch and investigate Briana.

The web was flat, ornate, and circular, the common type normally associated with spiders. "Look, Grandpa," Sammy said. "She has really long legs." I looked more closely and noticed that her body was about an inch long, but her legs were much longer. The spider was brightly colored, marked with yellow, black, and orange. The spider—that is, Briana—did not move much while we were observing her. I moved to place my finger on the web to see what it felt like. Sammy's response to my action was quick, "Don't touch her web, Grandpa, because she gets very upset." She asked me to move away from the web so she could show me how Briana was not afraid of her.

I watched as I moved back on the porch. Sammy moved slowly toward the web and then just stood there, motionless. In about a minute, though it seemed much longer, Briana slowly came down the web toward Sammy. I had to control myself to keep from yelling, "Sammy, that's amazing!" I never thought I would be watching a spider coming down a web toward my granddaughter without dispatching the spider. I asked Sammy if she had time to help me do a little Web searching to get more information about spiders.

Our first search was to find a little more about orb weavers. We found out that orb weavers are sometimes known as the black and yellow garden spider. The thick interwoven section in the web's center has also led to them being called the "writing spider." We continued on the Web site and learned that the male is often less than a quarter the size of the female and is normally not in the same web as the female. Orb weavers are harmless but can be a nuisance when they build their large webs across trails and other places inconvenient to humans.

The Web site reminded us that most spiders are small, inconspicuous arthropods and are harmless to humans. This caused Sammy to ask, "What's an arthropod?" I told her it means insects and spiders with jointed legs. We found out there are nearly 900 species of spiders in Texas and that only the recluse spider and black widow spider are considered poisonous to humans. We skipped down to black widows and were surprised to learn that contrary to popular belief, southern black widow female spiders do not eat their mates after mating. This is not true of their relatives to the north, where the clan got its name.

Thanks to Sammy, my concern over spiders was a thing of the past.

The Hoggs and Memorial Park

A friend and I had just arrived at Memorial Park (hike 1) for some hiking. As we got out of the car, my friend who is a history teacher said, "Did you know the family of 'Big Jim' Hogg deeded at cost, 1500 acres to the city to create this park in 1924? During World War I, the site contained Camp Logan, a training camp for soldiers."

My friend continued, "The Hogg children purchased the property with proceeds of the fortune they had amassed from the oil discovery in 1918 on their property, Varner Plantation. At one point in time they were earning $225,000 a month from the oil. According to Hogg biographer Gwendolyn Cone Neely, the Hoggs did not believe that the oil money was rightfully theirs, as it had come from the land and not hard work, and they were determined to use it for the good of Texas."

I replied that I had no idea that one family was responsible for this park, but I shared the knowledge I did have: "I know Memorial has nearly twice the acreage of New York's Central Park and ranks as the fifty-fifth largest city park in the country. It's also unique in that it has so many features, including the golf course, tennis courts, a jogging track, and acres of wooded hills for hiking and mountain biking. By the way, is Ima Hogg part of that family group? I often wondered why parents would ever give that name to a daughter."

My friend answered that he also had been curious about the name and had done a little research. He continued, "Her father, the aforementioned Big Jim Hogg, was responsible for the name and, believe it or not, was proud of it. After her birth on July 10, 1882, he wrote: 'Our cup of joy is now overflowing! We have a daughter of as fine proportions and of as angelic mien as ever gracious nature favor a man with, and her name is Ima!'"

I was taken aback. "I can't believe those words and that crude attempt to make them poetic came from a loving father." Despite that, Hogg served two terms as the twentieth governor of Texas, from 1890 to 1895. He was the first Texas governor who was born in the state.

"Apparently," my friend continued, "he had become fascinated with the name after seeing it in an epic poem, 'The Fate of Marvin,' written by his brother Thomas. The heroine of the poem was called Ima, short for Imogene."

Miss Hogg told the story: "My grandfather Stinson lived 15 miles from Mineola and news traveled slowly. When he learned of his granddaughter's name, he came trotting to town as fast as he could to protest, but it was too late. The christening had taken place, and Ima I was to remain." She endeavored to downplay her name by signing her first name illegibly and having her stationery printed with "I. Hogg" or "Miss Hogg." For decades she was considered to be the "First Lady of Texas." Her friends called her "Miss Ima." She never married and died in 1975.

Miss Ima had a significant impact on keeping Memorial Park a place for families and hikers, by appointing several of her friends to oversee the park: Terry Hershey, Frank C. Smith Jr.; Sadie Gwin Blackburn, and Dr. John D. Staub. They deflected hundreds of various misuses and development plans ranging from a fish hatchery to a university to oil exploration. The group became known as the Memorial Park Advisory Committee. They enforced the transfer agreement that stated the land must be used for park purposes only or it would revert to the Daughters of the Republic of Texas. The park is hugely popular and used by thousands of outdoor enthusiasts every year; in fact, the Memorial Park Conservancy received a 2006 Mayor's Proud Partner Award for significant trail improvements.

Houston Arboretum: Outer Loop

This well-marked loop trail skirts the perimeter of the arboretum and gives a taste of the variety of flora and fauna there. A short out-and-back path leads to Buffalo Bayou and a bird-watching platform. Depending on the season, it is possible to see an alligator near the bayou. This area has perfect habitat for birds, mammals, and snakes. The nature center at the trailhead is well worth visiting for its displays and hands-on exhibits.

Start: Willow Oak Trail, trailhead at east end of parking area

Distance: 2.5-mile loop with a short out and back

Approximate hiking time: 1.5 hours

Difficulty: Moderate due to lack of shade

Trail surface: Packed crushed gravel, boardwalks, dirt

Seasons: Year-round

Other trail users: Dog walkers, bird-watchers

Canine compatibility: Leashed dogs permitted

Fees and permits: None required; donations accepted and used to cover operating costs

Schedule: Winter, 8:30 a.m.–6 p.m.; summer, 8:30 a.m.–8 p.m.

Maps: Available in the park and online at www.houstonarboretum .org; USGS: Houston Heights

Trail contact: Houston Arboretum and Nature Center, 4501 Wood-way Dr., Houston 77024; (713) 681-8433; www.houston arboretum.org

Other: Restrooms and water are available at the visitor center. Joggers and cyclists are not allowed on trails. No picnicking or eating in the park (to protect wildlife).

Finding the trailhead: From the intersection of I-10 and Loop I-610 South, take Loop I-610 South to the Memorial Drive/ Woodway Drive exit 10. Turn left (east) at Woodway Drive and into the parking area at 4501 Woodway Dr. Parking is at the visitor center along the central driveway, as you enter the park. The trailhead adjoins the parking area. *DeLorme: Texas Atlas & Gazetteer:* Page 129, J10. GPS: N29 45.928' / W95 27.096'

THE HIKE

S tart the hike at the Willow Oak Trail trailhead located at the east end of the parking area. Head east toward the Outer Loop Trail. This hike combines sections of the Willow Oak Trail, the Outer Loop Trail, the out-and-back Charlotte Couch Birding Trail, and the Alice Brown Trail.

All of the trails are well marked, so it is easy to alter any hike as you go. Another advantage is that most of the trails are short, ranging in length from 400 feet to 0.5 mile. Boardwalks, mulch, and leaf-covered dirt make up the trail surface. Benches are placed strategically along the routes and are generally in the shade. Much of this hike is in the woods and well shaded, passing through forest, pond, and meadow habitats.

On the east side of the park, the Outer Loop Trail skirts the edge of a demonstration meadow. It consists of mostly grasses, sedges (rushlike plants), and wildflowers. Watch for sunflowers, asters, coreopsis, and Texas paintbrush, looking like

A great white egret feeding its young near Buffalo Bayou. The young are hatched in the spring each year.

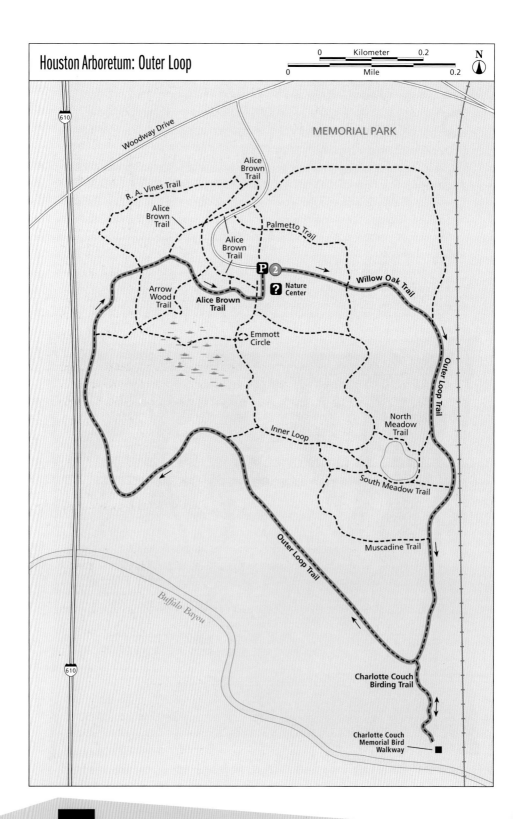

Houston Arboretum: Outer Loop

MEMORIAL PARK

Woodway Drive

R. A. Vines Trail

Alice Brown Trail

Alice Brown Trail

Alice Brown Trail

Palmetto Trail

Arrow Wood Trail

Alice Brown Trail

Nature Center

Willow Oak Trail

Emmott Circle

Outer Loop Trail

North Meadow Trail

Inner Loop

South Meadow Trail

Buffalo Bayou

Outer Loop Trail

Muscadine Trail

Charlotte Couch Birding Trail

Charlotte Couch Memorial Bird Walkway

N

0   Kilometer   0.2

0   Mile   0.2

a ragged brush dipped in bright paint. This is also a great place to look for some of the 167 species of birds found in the park, including killdeers, swallows, Carolina wrens, and the colorful eastern bluebirds. Red-tailed hawks may be observed perched in a tree, watching for a meal.

Nonvenomous water snakes reside near the pond, including the black-banded water snake, which is often mistaken for the water moccasin. Venomous water moccasins are in the park, but when found are moved to the bayou area. In the spring, listen for the sounds of green tree frogs, as groups of them form a noisy chorus.

Coyotes have moved into the park and are breeding here. It is unusual to see one, but you can add interest to the hike by watching for tracks. They are similar to a dog's print, except their front paw print is slightly larger than their back and shows four toes, while the back print is shaped like a pair of lips.

On the Charlotte Couch Bird Walkway overlooking Buffalo Bayou, at the end of the out-and-back leg of the hike, herons, egrets, and numerous songbirds may be seen. River birch, dogwood, and a variety of other tree species can also be found here.

Return to the Outer Loop and watch for southern red oaks, post oaks, large loblolly pines, southern magnolias, and numerous songbirds flitting in and out of the woods. Add another dimension to this hike by taking along binoculars or a field guide of your choice.

MILES AND DIRECTIONS

Note: All the trails are clearly identified with trail marker posts.

0.0 Start at the Willow Oak Trail trailhead at the east side of the parking area. Head due east on the trail.

0.1 In less than 0.1 mile reach the junction with the Palmetto Trail, which crosses the Willow Oak Trail from north to south. Continue east on Willow Oak.

0.2 Reach the T where the Willow Oak Trail ends at the Outer Loop Trail. Turn right onto the Outer Loop and follow it south.

> 🍃 **Green Tip:**
> *Avoid stepping on insects on the trail. Each has a specific purpose in maintaining a viable ecosystem.*

0.4 Bear left (southeast) and pass the North Meadow Trail on the right. Continue following the Outer Loop Trail around the meadow to the right, heading southeast and then bearing south.

0.5 Continue on the Outer Loop Trail as it passes the South Meadow Trail to the right (west). A sign states TO POND (GPS: N29 45.687' / W95 26.954').

0.6 Continue following the Outer Loop Trail south and pass the Muscadine Trail on the right (west). Bear slightly left (east) while following the Outer Loop.

0.8 Reach a wooden bench and a sign on the left that states CHARLOTTE COUCH BIRDING TRAIL. Turn left onto the narrow path, heading south/southeast. This is a short out and back.

1.0 The boardwalk leads up to the Charlotte Couch Memorial Bird Walkway. The wooden platform overlooks Buffalo Bayou, and a sign warns of the presence of alligators. Backtrack to where you left the Outer Loop Trail.

1.2 Reach the T with the Outer Loop Trail and turn left, heading west. Follow the trail as it bends right (northwest).

1.4 Pass a semicircular clearing on the right that is about 60 feet across and 30 feet deep.

1.7 Reach a junction on the right where a short connector trail leads east to the Inner Loop Trail (GPS: N29 45.743' / W95 27.159'). Continue on the Outer Loop Trail, making a sweeping semicircle to the left and heading southwest, and then bend right, heading north.

2.1 Reach a junction on the right (east) with Arrow Wood Trail. Continue following the Outer Loop as it heads north and then bends hard right, heading east.

2.3 Reach the junction where the R. A. Vines Trail crosses the Outer Loop Trail from north to south. Continue following the Outer Loop as it bears east.

2.4 Reach the junction where the Alice Brown Trail crosses the Outer Loop Trail. Turn right onto Alice Brown, heading southeast. Cross over the Arrow Wood Trail and continue following the Alice Brown Trail.

2.5 End the hike at the back of the nature center and return to the parking area.

Houston Arboretum: Inner Loop

This hike is great for nature lovers and families. The several well-marked interconnecting loops pass by a small pond full of life, over boardwalks, and through a swamp, heavy woods, and a meadow area. This is the perfect habitat for birds, mammals, and snakes. The arboretum is on the site of Camp Logan, which was active from 1917 to 1923 during World War I. Armadillos occasionally dig up Camp Logan artifacts while searching for food.

Start: Behind nature center at Alice Brown Trail trailhead
Distance: 1.4 miles of interconnecting loops
Approximate hiking time: 1 hour
Difficulty: Easy due to level terrain
Trail surface: Boardwalks, packed gravel, mulch, dirt
Seasons: Year-round
Other trail users: Bird-watchers, dog walkers
Canine compatibility: Leashed dogs permitted
Fees and permits: None required; donations accepted and used to cover operating costs
Schedule: Winter, 8:30 a.m.–6 p.m.; summer, 8:30 a.m.–8 p.m.
Maps: Available in the park and online at www.houston arboretum.org/hours.asp and www.houstonarboretum.org/propertymap.asp; USGS: Houston Heights.
Trail contact: Houston Arboretum and Nature Center, 4501 Woodway Dr., Houston 77024; (713) 681-8433; www.houston arboretum.org
Other: Restrooms and water are available at the visitor center. Joggers and cyclists are not allowed on trails. No picnicking or eating in the park (to protect wildlife).

Finding the trailhead: From the intersection of I-10 and Loop I-610 South, take Loop I-610 South to the Memorial Drive/Woodway Drive exit 10. Turn left at Woodway Drive and into the parking area at 4501 Woodway Dr. Parking is at the visitor center along the central driveway. The trailhead is at the rear of the nature center. *DeLorme: Texas Atlas & Gazetteer:* Page 129, J10. GPS: N29 45.904' / W95 27.127'

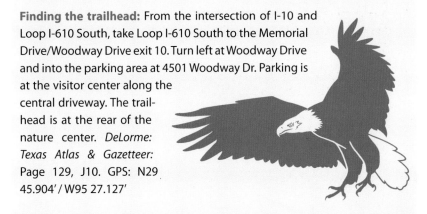

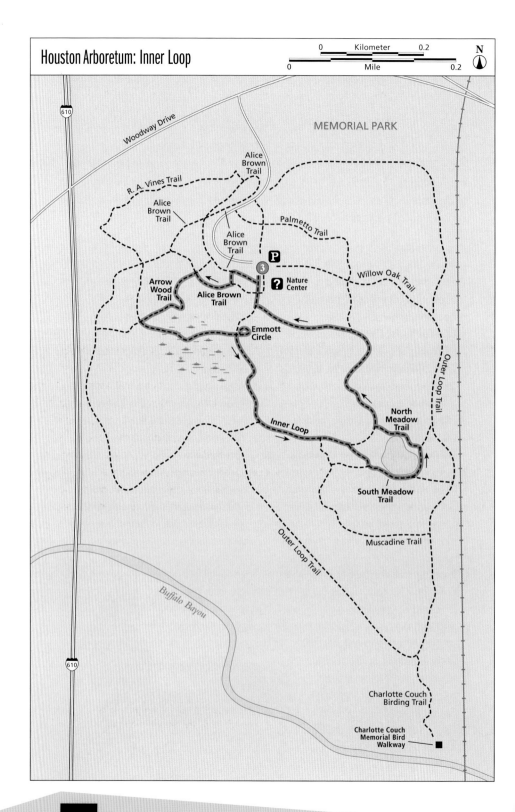

Houston Arboretum: Inner Loop

Kilometer 0 0.2

Mile 0 0.2

N

MEMORIAL PARK

610

Woodway Drive

Alice Brown Trail

R. A. Vines Trail

Alice Brown Trail

Alice Brown Trail

Palmetto Trail

Willow Oak Trail

P

3

Nature Center

Arrow Wood Trail

Alice Brown Trail

Emmott Circle

Outer Loop Trail

North Meadow Trail

Inner Loop

South Meadow Trail

Muscadine Trail

Outer Loop Trail

Buffalo Bayou

610

Charlotte Couch Birding Trail

Charlotte Couch Memorial Bird Walkway

THE HIKE

Start this hike behind the nature center at the trailhead for the Alice Brown Trail. This first portion of the hike is wheelchair and stroller accessible. Pick up a trail map at the nature center. Benches are placed strategically and are generally in the shade. Much of the hike is in the woods and well shaded. Depending on the time of the year, mosquitoes can be pesky, so be prepared.

Portions of the Alice Brown Trail, the Arrow Wood Trail, the R. A. Vines Trail, and the Inner Loop Trail will be explored. All of the trails are well marked, so it is easy to alter the hike as you go. The swamp area, reached on the R. A. Vines Trail, is teeming with wildlife. The trail is named in honor of Robert A. Vines, a local ecologist who during the 1950s advocated using a section of Memorial Park as a nature sanctuary.

Enjoy the sounds of the swamp, including the deep *jug-o-rum* of the bullfrog, the largest frog in North America. Red-eared slider turtles may be basking on logs but will quickly slide into the water when they sense vibrations from walkers.

Watch for dragonflies, with their ability to hover in one spot while hunting for mosquitoes. Ribbon snakes, which may reach 2 feet in length, like to be near the edge of the water. These nonvenomous, fast-moving snakes feast on salamanders, frogs, and insects. Nonvenomous black-banded water snakes, often mistaken for venomous water moccasins, swim in the water. The park staff move any water moccasins they find on the trails to the area around the bayou. The swamp cyrilla, a shrub, thrives in the wet conditions. It stays green most of the year and produces little white flowers that have a lot of nectar to attract bees.

The horned lizard is the Texas state reptile. The armadillo is the official state small mammal.

On the Inner Loop Trail, listen for the drumming of woodpeckers. Watch for the six species of these colorful birds found in the park, ranging from the size of a small fist to the size of a crow. Altogether, there are 167 species of birds in the park.

This trail presents a good sampling of the more than 100 species of trees and shrubs growing in the park. Oaks are common, with 12 species represented, including the evergreen, live oak, southern red oak, and post oak. Make a game out of trying to identify the acorns. Pass by loblolly pines, dogwoods, ash magnolias, and sycamores. Add another dimension to your hike by taking along your favorite field guide.

A boardwalk crosses this swamp on the Inner Loop Trail. This area is alive with plants, frogs, birds, and sometimes a snake.

MILES AND DIRECTIONS

Note: All the trails are clearly identified with trail marker posts.

0.0 Start at the sidewalk at the rear of the nature center, then follow the board-walk through several displays.

0.1 Reach a Y at the Alice Brown Trail trailhead. Take the left branch, heading south, and then bear right (west).

0.2 Reach a junction where the Arrow Wood Trail crosses the Alice Brown Trail. Turn left, going south on Arrow Wood. In a couple hundred yards, pass a small pond on the left surrounded by a boardwalk. Continue following the Arrow Wood Trail south.

0.3 Reach a junction with the R. A. Vines Trail. Turn left, heading east on R. A. Vines, and follow the trail and boardwalks through the swamp area.

0.5 Reach a junction where the Inner Loop Trail crosses the R. A. Vines Trail. Continue following R. A. Vines across the Inner Loop, then follow left around Emmott Circle back to the junction. Go left onto the Inner Loop, heading south.

0.6 Pass a connector path on the right to the Outer Loop Trail. Bear left, following the Inner Loop east.

0.7 Pass a connector path on the right to the Muscadine Trail. Continue following the Inner Loop east.

0.8 Reach a Y and take the right branch onto the South Meadow Trail, heading southeast.

0.9 Bear left on the trail and pass a pond with a boardwalk. Follow as the trail turns and heads north to a T. Take the left branch west onto the North Meadow Trail.

1.0 Reach a T where the North Meadow Trail ends. Take the right branch, heading north onto the Inner Loop Trail.

1.2 Bear left (west) before reaching a junction on the right where the Palmetto Trail dead-ends into the Inner Loop Trail. Continue heading west on the Inner Loop.

1.3 Reach a connector path on the right that leads north, back to the nature center.

1.4 End the hike at the rear of the nature center.

Buffalo Bayou: Tinsley Trail

This hike has a split personality. The Houston skyline is to the north, Allen Parkway and Memorial Drive serve as north and south borders, and in between is the park with a large greenbelt area and Buffalo Bayou meandering through it. Sections of the hike offer a retreat from the hustle and bustle of the city while still within it.

Start: Trailhead adjacent to northeast side of Tinsley Park parking area

Distance: 2.4 miles out and back

Approximate hiking time: 1.5 hours

Difficulty: Easy due to paved trail and minor elevation changes

Trail surface: Concrete, asphalt

Seasons: Year-round

Other trail users: Dog walkers, joggers, cyclists, and mountain bikers

Canine compatibility: Leashed dogs permitted

Fees and permits: None required

Schedule: 6 a.m.–11 p.m.

Maps: None available in the park; USGS: Houston Heights.

Trail contact: Houston Parks and Recreation Department (HPARD), 2999 South Wayside Dr., Houston 77023; (713) 865-4500; www .houstontx.gov/parks/trails.html

Other: Many high-attendance events are held here; call in advance for schedule, as the park can be crowded and parking difficult. There are no restrooms along the trail.

Finding the trailhead: Traveling south on I-45 toward downtown, take the Allen Parkway exit on the left (exit 47A). Pass Sabine Street, and the park entrance is immediately on the right. Turn right into the parking lot at 500 Allen Pkwy. *DeLorme: Texas Atlas & Gazetteer:* Page 130, J2. GPS: N29 45.702' / W95 22.758'

E leanor Tinsley Park is located southwest of downtown, within the Sabine-to-Taft greenway. It is named in honor of city councilwoman Eleanor Tinsley, who served from 1980 to 1990. The trailhead is off the northeast corner of the parking lot. The park is the site of major festivals and events, including the city's Fourth of July fireworks extravaganza.

Start at the sidewalk with a short out-and-back hike down to the bayou. Follow the trail as it slopes down and doubles back on itself, then straightens out and leads to the edge of the water. There is a landing from which canoes may be launched. Interesting retaining walls, made from stone, follow the slope. A children's playground is located in the greenspace.

Backtrack and follow the sidewalk west to the sign at the trailhead marked BIKE ROUTE. This is a multiuse trail, so stay to the right and be alert to mountain bikers. Buffalo Bayou is down a slope to the right, and Allen Parkway is on the left. Trees line Allen Parkway, including some large live oaks, but the traffic noise can be distracting.

The interior of the park consists of greenspace, mostly mowed grass, and many trees, including oak, sycamore, and magnolia. The bayou meanders through the center, and benches are placed along the trail. This is also one of a few hikes where fire hydrants are found along the trail—now that's different!

Several trails in the Houston Park system have world-famous sculptures. This huge red sculpture, by Mac Whitney, is entitled *Houston*.

Buffalo Bayou: Tinsley Trail

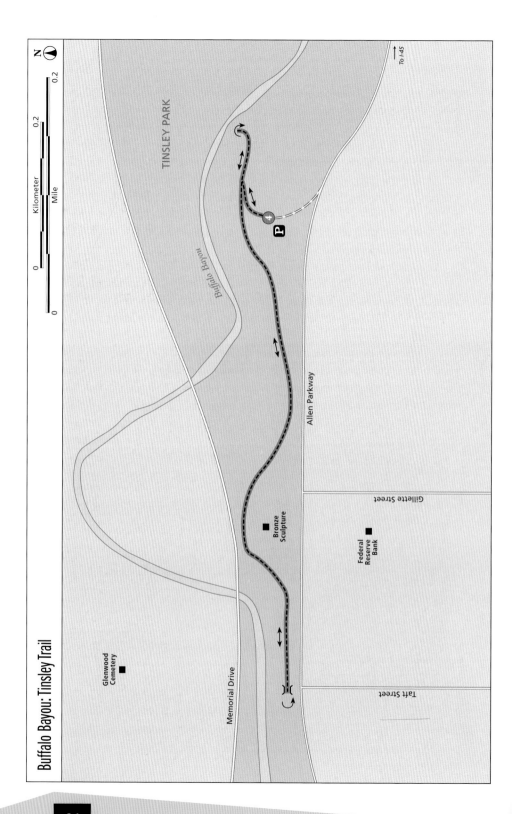

The trail passes through both open and shaded tree canopy. The bayou is still to the right and generally about 40 feet away, down a slope. There are sections where it's possible to get to the edge of the bayou. When backtracking, great views of downtown Houston are available.

Pass an imposing brown structure on the left, across Allen Parkway. This is the Houston branch of the Federal Reserve Bank. The nine-acre complex consists of seven buildings.

Next, pass a large bronze sculpture on the left. Titled *Large Spindle Piece,* it's a 12-foot-tall piece of abstract art by Henry Moore (1898–1986). The sculpture was purchased by the Knox Foundation and given to the city in 1979. It had been located in England, in London's Hyde Park.

The Police Officers Memorial can be seen to the right, across Memorial Drive. The design of the pyramid-shaped concrete monument is Mayan-inspired, and a pool of bubbling water flows down from the top. End your hike after reaching the bridge at Taft Street and backtrack to the trailhead.

MILES AND DIRECTIONS

0.0 Start at the trailhead adjacent to the northeast side of the Tinsley Park parking area.

0.1 Continue following the trail (sidewalk) as its bends back on itself and slopes down toward the bayou.

0.2 Reach the bank of Buffalo Bayou. Canoes may be launched from this point. Backtrack to the trailhead and parking area to continue the hike.

0.3 Reach the Y and follow trail right to the bike route sign (GPS: N29 45.689' / W95 22.820'). Allen Parkway is on the left, about 60 feet away.

0.5 Continue following the concrete trail west. Allen Parkway is on the left, with greenspace and the bayou visible on the right.

0.6 Continue following the trail as it bends right, away from Allen Parkway.

0.7 The imposing Federal Reserve Bank building and complex is directly across Allen Parkway.

0.9 The trail changes from concrete sidewalk to asphalt and bears toward the bayou on the right. The Henry Moore sculpture is on the left.

1.0 The trail passes the Channel 11–KHOU building on the left (south), with a helicopter landing pad on its roof.

1.2 Cross over the Taft Tributary flowing into Buffalo Bayou on a short footbridge and then bear right, heading north for a short way.

1.4 Heading west on the trail, pass under a concrete bridge at Taft Street. The trail continues west, but at this point turn around and retrace your steps for 0.3 mile.

1.7 Bear left (northeast) of the concrete trail onto a narrow dirt trail created by mountain bikers. This path follows the south edge of the bayou and is parallel to the main trail (GPS: N29 45.675′ / W95 23.326′).

1.8 Follow the bike path along the bayou and up a slope to rejoin the concrete trail. Backtrack to the trailhead.

2.4 End the hike at the trailhead and return to the parking area.

Trailside Sculptures

A number of the hikes in Houston parks have world-famous sculptures placed along the trail. Included in these is *Upside Down Canoe,* by John Runnels, a Houston-based artist. These silver stainless-steel canoes, part of a trellis, are placed at several of the street-level entrances to the Buffalo Bayou trails. Henry Moore's 12-foot-tall bronze abstract, *Large Spindle Piece,* is on the Buffalo Bayou's Tinsley Trail. Mac Whitney's huge red sculpture, called *Houston,* is located on the White Oak Bayou Hike and Bike Trail. These sculptures are indeed strange items to see while hiking, but offer a different type of scenery.

Buffalo Bayou: Blue Lagoon Trail

This trail is downtown and located in the 23-acre Sabine to Bagby Waterfront Park. It is one of the few trails that are best to hike at night, due to its signature lighting system. The lights change colors from white to blue based on the phases of the moon. Much of the hike is below street level and passes the Entertainment District as it explores both sides of Buffalo Bayou. The trail may be followed to Allen's Landing, the spot where the Allen brothers landed in 1836 and founded Houston.

Start: Southeast corner of city parking lot H at Blue Lagoon Trail trailhead
Distance: 2.4-mile loop with an out and back
Approximate hiking time: 1.5 hours
Difficulty: Moderate due to some stairs and rough trail sections
Trail surface: Concrete
Seasons: Year-round
Other trail users: Dog walkers, cyclists, tourists
Canine compatibility: Leashed dogs permitted

Fees and permits: None required
Schedule: 6 a.m.–11 p.m.
Maps: None available in the park, but online at www.buffalobayou .org/sabinebagby.html; USGS: Settegast
Trail contact: Houston Parks and Recreation Department (HPARD), 2999 South Wayside Dr., Houston 77023; (713) 865-4500; www .houstontx.gov/parks/trails.html
Other: There are no restroom facilities on the hike, but the aquarium complex allows hikers to use its restrooms.

Finding the trailhead: Traveling south on I-45 toward downtown, take the Allen Parkway exit on the left (exit 47A). Turn right onto Sabine Street and go 1 block to city parking lot H. *DeLorme: Texas Atlas & Gazetteer:* Page 130, J2. GPS: N29 45.754' / W95 22.441'

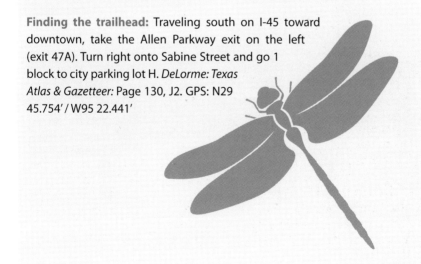

THE HIKE

Start the hike from city parking lot H. The Blue Lagoon Trail, aka the Sabine to Bagby Promenade, was opened in June 2006. Much of the trail is wheelchair and stroller accessible. This is a multiuse trail, so stay to the right and watch for cyclists and joggers. There are benches along the trail.

The trail's signature element is the cobalt blue and white lights that line its entire length and at night illuminate the bayou. The lights shift with the phases of the moon. On each full moon, all the lights are white, and then, traveling from east to west, change to blue until they are all blue for the new moon. There's also blue and white lighting of the trees, which makes for a spectacular visual. This lighting has created a new opportunity for hiking at night.

Daytime hiking is also visually pleasant due to the 300,000 plants and 600 native trees that line the banks of the bayou. The trail weaves through willow, oak, river birch, sycamore, magnolia, dogwood, and many other tree species. Shrubs

> *Sam Houston (1793–1863) served as governor of Tennessee from 1827 to 1831. He then moved to Texas and became its governor from 1859 to 1861.*

These upside-down canoe sculptures, by John Runnels, greet hikers at five of the street-level entrances to the Buffalo Bayou trails.

and groundcover reaching down to the edge of the water are attention-getting. Birds, including songbirds and white egrets, enjoy the water. Sections of the trail are below I-45, which furnishes additional shade . . . and noise.

The trail has five entries, called portals, that invite hikers into the park. Each portal has a raised 20-foot, stainless-steel, upside-down canoe sculpture that serves as a bayou landmark. Folks can walk under them as they enter the park— now that's something different!

The Downtown Aquarium, just before the Bagby Street bridge, features a 500,000-gallon aquarium, dining, and an amusement park. It is located on the north side of the bayou and can be reached from the trail. The Entertainment District is on the south side of the bayou and includes the Wortham Center, where the Houston Ballet and Grand Opera perform. The Hobby Center for the Performing Arts is also on the south side.

The pedestrian bridge, 189 feet long and 10 feet wide, has space for hikers, joggers, cyclists, and tourists. It provides access to both banks of the bayou without having to cross any streets. The view from the center of the bridge provides a good photo op.

After reaching the University of Houston, enjoy a great view of downtown. Then backtrack to the trailhead, possibly enjoying a meal along the way.

MILES AND DIRECTIONS

0.0   Start at the Buffalo Bayou North Trail connector path at the sign at the southeast corner of city parking lot H. Turn left (east) at the T.

0.1   Pass a brick path on the right that leads to the edge of the bayou. I-45 is directly overhead.

0.2   Reach a Y and take the left branch, labeled LOWER TRAIL. This is closer to the bayou and will reconnect with the right branch. It also passes under the 189-foot-long wooden pedestrian bridge that connects both sides of the bayou. You will return on this bridge.

0.3   Pass a portal (entrance) with stairs leading to Memorial Drive. The upside-down canoe sculpture is visible.

0.4   Pass a stairway on the right leading down to the bayou.

0.5   Pass a stairway on the left leading up to the Downtown Aquarium entertainment complex. Restrooms and water are available.

Buffalo Bayou: Blue Lagoon Trail

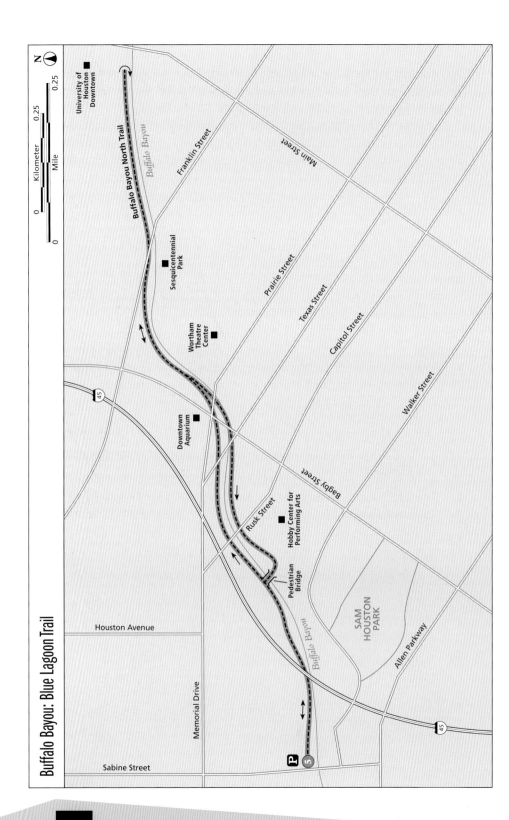

0.6 Reach a Y. Take the right branch, which leads under the Bagby Street bridge. This is the end of the Blue Lagoon Trail and its lights. Sesquicentennial Park begins at this point (GPS: N29 45.839′ / W95 22.018′).

0.7 Cross a short wooden bridge that spans a drainage channel that leads to the bayou. Continue following the trail.

0.8 Go under a bridge and bear left, following the trail.

0.9 I-45 is above the trail, and there are many concrete support pilings around the trail.

1.0 The University of Houston–Downtown Branch can be seen immediately ahead. The Spaghetti Warehouse is ahead and to the right.

1.2 The trail ends at the University of Houston, which is on the left. Go up seven flights of stairs to the street-level University Plaza. The view of downtown Houston is great. Backtrack to the Bagby Street bridge and the portal to the street.

1.8 Cross the bridge to the south side of Buffalo Bayou. Turn right and follow the Blue Lagoon Trail. The bayou is on the right, and the Downtown Aquarium is across the bayou.

2.0 Pass under the Capitol Street bridge and stairs on the left leading up to Capitol Street.

2.1 The Hobby Center parking building is on the left.

2.2 Reach the wooden pedestrian bridge. Turn right onto the bridge and cross over the bayou to the Upper Trail. Turn left onto the Upper Trail and backtrack to the trailhead.

2.4 Reach the trailhead and return to city parking lot H.

The Founding and Settling of Houston

In 1836 two enterprising New York real estate promoters took a canoe up and down Buffalo Bayou, in what is now Texas. They were searching for vacant land to fulfill their dream of establishing "a great center of government and commerce." In August, Augustus and John Allen found the location they were looking for. It was near the confluence of Buffalo Bayou and White Oak Bayou and presented a natural turning basin for boats. This spot is now known as Allen's Landing and has been restored by the City of Houston. It can be reached on Hike 5.

Paddling down the uncharted Buffalo Bayou was quite adventurous as it was not know what was around each bend. It was also potentially dangerous, since just four months earlier, on April 21, General Sam Houston had defeated Mexican general Santa Ana at the Battle of San Jacinto, about 40 miles from where the Allen brothers landed. To the folks living in Texas, the battle cry of "Remember the Alamo!" and the crushing defeat of General Santa Ana avenged the Mexican slaughter at the Alamo. It also was the foundation for creating the new Republic of Texas.

With this background, the Allen brothers researched the area and found out the 6,642 acres were part of a land grant given to John Austin. Austin was one of the original group of U.S. citizens given land grants by the Mexican government. The land was now owned by Mrs. T. Parrot, the widow of John Austin. Money was hard to come by, and she sold it to the brothers for $9,428—that's about $1.40 an acre. The brothers named the new city Houston after General Sam Houston, whom they admired and felt would become the republic's president. Gail Borden Jr., a publisher and surveyor who later founded Borden, Inc., was hired by the Allens to lay out the city.

Houston started out as a frontier hamlet, built on the ashes of Harrisburg, which had been destroyed during the war. The city was incorporated on June 5, 1837, and made the temporary capital. (Austin became the permanent capital in 1844.) The Allen brothers' dream was starting to materialize, but unfortunately, growth fostered lawlessness, disease, and financial difficulties, which were quickly growing into severe problems. By January 1840 a few creditors had already stopped lending and cut off some Houston businessmen. Numerous yellow fever epidemics added to the troubles. The yellow fever outbreaks were intensified by the fact that most transportation was on rivers and bayous, which supported huge quantities of mosquitoes. About 12 percent of the city's population died from yellow fever in 1839. These outbreaks continued until after the Civil War in the 1860s.

Later in 1840 the Allen brothers started to seriously promote their town, at the same time that the republic started promoting the settling of Texas. The Allens misled prospective buyers with advertisements boasting of waterfalls and grassy plains, when all Houston had were bayous. But the brothers, along with influential Houston businessmen, really wanted their city to succeed. Despite the many problems, Houston did get several projects funded very quickly. Included in these was digging a channel for the proposed Port of Houston. It began on January 19, 1842, when Congress approved a move to dig out the Buffalo Bayou. It would take decades to complete this project, known as the Ship Channel. A railroad system was started during the 1850s, and by 1860 450 miles of track were laid. The majority of the track-laying was done by Mexicans, who were among the first immigrants to Houston. Houston was on the move.

Buffalo Bayou: Sabine to Waugh

Explore 2 miles on the north side of Buffalo Bayou, just west of downtown Houston. Good views of the downtown skyline are available. There is much greenspace, and the edges of the bayou have a wide variety of tree species. Reach the Waugh Drive bridge, home to 250,000 Mexican free-tailed bats. They're quite a sight as they leave their roost en masse around dusk.

Start: Southeast corner of city parking lot H
Distance: 4.4 miles out and back
Approximate hiking time: 2.75 hours
Difficulty: Moderate due to length and lack of shade
Trail surface: Asphalt, concrete
Seasons: Year-round
Other trail users: Mountain bikers, cyclists, joggers, dog walkers
Canine compatibility: Leashed dogs permitted

Fees and permits: None required
Schedule: 6 a.m.–11 p.m.
Maps: None available in the park; USGS: Settegast
Trail contact: Houston Parks and Recreation Department (HPARD), 2999 South Wayside Dr., Houston 77023; (713) 865-4500; www .houstontx.gov/parks/trails.html
Other: There are no restroom facilities on the trail.

Finding the trailhead: Traveling north on I-45 toward downtown, take the Allen Parkway exit on the left (exit 47A). Turn right onto Sabine Street and continue to city parking lot H. *DeLorme: Texas Atlas & Gazetteer:* Page 130, J2. GPS: N29 45.754' / W95 22.441'

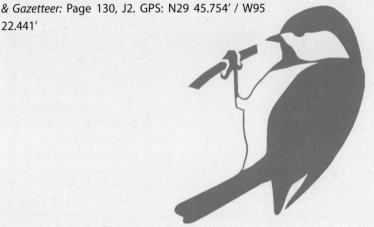

THE HIKE

Start the hike from city parking lot H. Follow the connector path at the southeast corner to the T and take the right (west) branch. The trail is wheelchair and stroller accessible. This is a multiuse trail, so stay to the right and watch for mountain bikers, cyclists, and joggers. There are benches along the trail. The tree canopy is intermittent, but furnishes some shade. Take a hat, sunscreen, and water.

This very short part of the trail, between the trailhead and Sabine Street is technically part of the Blue Bayou Trail. Enter the Art Park, a small grassy area around the trail where sculptures and other artwork by local artists are displayed. The sidewalk sections are painted alternately blue and white, displaying a poem. Reach the portal (entrance) to Sabine Street. At the entrance on the right, a raised 20-foot, stainless-steel, upside-down canoe sculpture that serves as a bayou landmark can be seen. Continue west, going under the Sabine Street bridge.

> *The bark of the black willow tree contains salicylic acid, which is used to make aspirin. Native Americans used this bark much as we do aspirin today.*

On the Sabine to Waugh Trail, hikers can see the Houston skyline and fire hydrants.

Buffalo Bayou: Sabine to Waugh

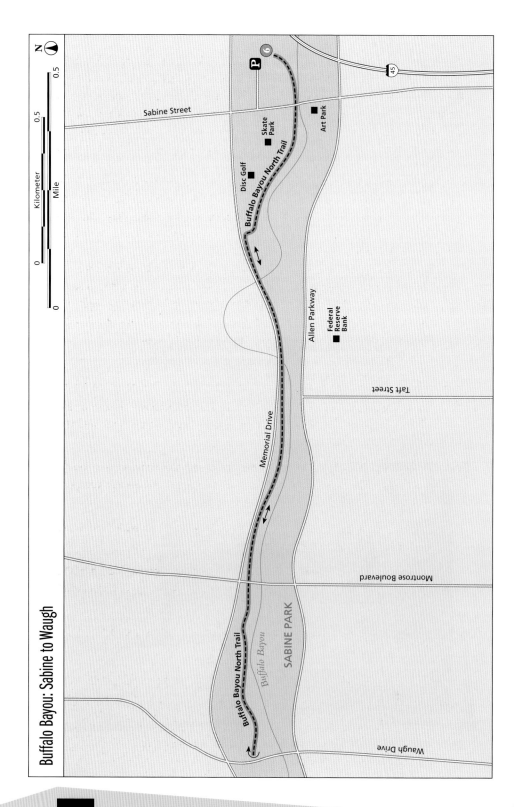

The left edge of the trail slopes down about 25 feet to the bayou. To the right and left of the trail the greenspace is mostly mowed grass, with bushes and trees at the water's edge. Eleanor Tinsley Park can be seen to the left, across the bayou. Up a slope and on the right side is the Lee and Joe Jamail Skate Park and adjoining it is the Jim Mozola Memorial Disc Golf area. The trail follows the bayou as it makes a lazy bend to the right. Willows, live oaks, sycamores, and other trees line the water's edge.

Reach a sidewalk on the right and follow it, taking a short out-and–back walk into a small section of woods. A drainage channel lined with rocks and concrete leads to the bayou. Maidenhair ferns and wildflowers create a pleasant palette, and benches and large rocks are available to sit on. This is a great, peaceful, shaded area to have a snack. Backtrack to the main trail and turn right.

Continue following the curves and bends as the trail heads west. On the left there is a large group of live oak trees with their branches touching the ground. Inhale, but not too deeply. The slightly unpleasant aroma is from the guano (droppings) of the 250,000 Mexican free-tailed bats that roost under the Waugh Drive bridge. This is a good spot to stop and backtrack to the trailhead.

MILES AND DIRECTIONS

0.0 Start at the Buffalo Bayou North Trail connector path at the sign at the southeast corner of city parking lot H. At the T, turn right (west) onto the trail.

0.1 Go through the Art Park, with a few scattered exhibits. Pass the portal (entrance) on the right with stairs to Sabine Street. Continue following the trail and pass under the Sabine Street bridge.

0.2 Pass the Lee and Joe Jamail Skate Park and the Jim Mozola Memorial Disc Golf area, both on the right.

0.4 Turn right where a sidewalk joins the trail. This is a short out-and-back hike in and out of woods. Stop before reaching the buildings and backtrack (GPS: N29 45.762' / W95 22.732').

0.5 Reach the T at the main trail. Turn right (west) and follow the trail.

> **🌿 Green Tip:**
> *If you're toting food, leave the packaging at home. Repack your provisions in ziplock bags that you can reuse and that can double as garbage bags on the way out of the woods.*

0.6 Reach and cross a short wooden footbridge over the Tapley Tributary, which flows to the bayou.

0.9 Bend left in a semicircle and follow along the bayou. The imposing three-story brown Federal Reserve Bank building can be seen directly to the left, across the bayou and Allen Parkway.

1.0 Continue west on the trail. On the left side pass by the back of the Police Officers Memorial.

1.1 Bend to the right, away from the bayou, and go under the Memorial Drive bridge.

1.2 Reach a bike path joining the trail on the left. The bridge is still above. Turn left (south) onto the bike path as it leads away from the bridge to the bayou, then bear right (west) and follow the path until it joins the main trail.

1.3 Reach the main trail coming from the right and continue west.

1.7 Continue following the trail west. Pass under a bridge crossing the bayou, joining Allen Parkway and Memorial Drive.

1.9 Continue following the trail west and pass a bench and exercise station with a "chinning" bar. Then cross a wooden platform bridge over a tributary to Buffalo Bayou.

2.1 Bear left (south), then straight ahead and bear right (west). The Waugh Drive bridge is in view. There is a water fountain to the right of the trail.

2.2 Pass a group of very large live oaks on the left. Reach the Waugh Drive bridge, home to 250,000 bats! Stop at this point (GPS: N29 45.763' / W95 23.851'), then backtrack to the trailhead.

4.4 Reach the trailhead and return to city parking lot H.

Bats at the Bridge

After finishing the 2-mile hike along Buffalo Bayou from Sabine to Waugh (hike 6), I asked my friend, a biologist, if he wanted to see the neighbors go out for dinner. We moseyed over to the Waugh Drive Bridge in the late afternoon to watch the 300,000-strong bat colony leave the roost.

Unlike other Texas bat colonies that migrate south in winter, the Waugh Bridge colony remains in Houston throughout the year. My friend told me, "When bats are mentioned, people often think of vampires, Halloween, and scary movies, but discounting the folklore and myths, they're an important group of animals. There are two main types of bats comprising nearly 1,000 different species. One is the large 'flying foxes' that eat fruit and the other is the smaller insect-eating bats, like these Mexican free-tailed bats."

The bats started to leave the roost on their daily search for food. They dropped down from the crevices in the bridge and then headed upward. It was an awesome sight as they began to fill the sky. My friend explained that the bats stay out all night hunting, and when they return in the morning, each bat will have gorged on 500 to 1,000 insects, including mosquitoes, each hour. I commented, "That's an amazing number. I can't even imagine what that number would be if you multiplied it by 8 hours and then by 300,000."

Then I asked if bats can see at night and how they find the insects. He told me that bats have excellent night vision, but their main tool is that they can also "see" with sound. This is called "echolocation." Bats that use echolocation usually have large ears and leaf-shaped flaps of skin on their noses. Their ears are wide and set apart to help direct the high frequency sounds they make to help them locate their next meal.

While we had our heads cocked back to watch their exit from the bridge, a solitary bat fell to the ground about 10 yards from us. A family with young children was closer. The children were curious and started toward the bat. My friend and I called out, "Don't go near that bat!" We went over to the parents who had been startled by our yelling and explained to them that people should not handle bats that are on the ground, because they may be sick. Bats can carry rabies, a very dangerous disease, and can transmit it to humans.

My friend took this opportunity to note the size of the dead bat. He said the Mexican free-tailed bat is a medium-size bat, with a wingspan of 12 to 14 inches, weighing between 0.4 and 0.5 ounce (Yes! Half an ounce!). They may live up to eighteen years. He pointed out the animal's wings or "hands," which have very long finger bones. I also saw that the bat had brown fur, a mammalian characteristic. Then we returned to watching the bats.

My friend continued to fill me in on bat info: "I imagine you know that bats are 'warm-blooded.' They generally give birth to one baby each summer and nurse their young, which are called pups, with milk. They are the only mammals that can fly and are the official state flying mammal of Texas." He said their colonies are the largest communities of mammals in the world.

The young roost separately from their mothers in the highest reaches of the roost, where temperatures are the warmest. The mothers leave the babies behind while they go out to hunt insects. It would seem that a bat mother would have trouble locating her baby among the thousands in the colony. It is believed that she remembers generally where she left her pup. Then after searching only a few minutes, she recognizes its cry and smell. Imagine trying to do that! In another way though they are not very good mothers, for if a baby falls from the roost, the mother will not come to its rescue. This gives predators the opportunity for a quick meal.

Most Mexican free-tailed bats live in caves—not under bridges—in the southern United States, most notably Texas. In 2006 a bat observation deck was installed at the corner of Waugh Drive and Allen Street to provide easier viewing of this particular colony.

At this point, it appeared that most of the bats were out from under the bridge, happily munching bugs, and my mind was going into information overflow mode. "Going out for dinner" will never be quite the same.

Hermann Park

This is a great hike for the entire family. The enlarged McGovern Lake includes three new islands supplying wetland habitat. There are many amenities for young hikers, including a miniature train ride and the Houston Zoo. These are advantages a city hike can offer over a country hike. Philanthropist George Hermann gave Houston 285 acres for the park in May 1914. It is the city's most developed park, and with over five million visitors, one of the most visited.

Start: Crushed-gravel trail adjacent to parking lot
Distance: 1.8-mile loop
Approximate hiking time: 1 hour
Difficulty: Easy due to flat paved trails
Trail surface: Crushed packed granite, concrete
Seasons: Year-round
Other trail users: Dog walkers, wheelchairs, strollers, cyclists, joggers
Canine compatibility: Leashed dogs permitted

Fees and permits: None required
Schedule: 6 a.m.–11 p.m.
Maps: None available in the park; USGS: Bellaire
Trail contact: Houston Parks and Recreation Department (HPARD), 2999 South Wayside Dr., Houston 77023; (713) 865-4500; www .houstontx.gov/parks/trails.html
Other: Water fountains are scattered throughout the park. Restrooms are located at the Miller Outdoor Theatre.

Finding the trailhead: From Memorial Park turn left onto Memorial Drive, then make an easy left onto Woodway Drive. After 0.5 mile turn left onto the West Loop Freeway North. Merge onto I-610 South and, in less than 2 miles, merge onto US 59 North at exit 8A toward downtown. Take the Main Street exit. Keep straight to go onto Wentworth Street. Follow Wentworth to Fannin Street and turn right. Turn into Hermann Park, north off Fannin Street. *DeLorme: Texas Atlas & Gazetteer:* Page 134, B1. GPS: N29 43.254' / W95 23.506'

THE HIKE

There is no official trailhead. Use the north entrance parking lot and cross the sidewalk to the wide crushed-gravel trail and turn right. The trail has no signs, but it is virtually impossible to get lost. It is wheelchair and stroller accessible and is lighted for hiking after dusk. The Texas Medical Center is on the southwest edge of the park, so occasionally a helicopter may be heard.

The children's train crosses the trail numerous times, winding its way around the park. This is a "people-person park," as there are always hikers, walkers, joggers, tourists, and generally a busload of schoolchildren. This combined with all the amenities make it an interesting hike.

Pass near a fenced area on the left that encloses the Japanese Garden. For this short section of the hike, Fannin Street will be on the right. The trail bears generally left or straight ahead. Large live oak trees are scattered along the trail, many with Spanish moss trailing from them. In the spring of 1920, the War Mothers of Houston planted 240 oak trees around the park to honor Harris County soldiers killed in World War I. Many of these trees furnish shade today.

> ***Native Americans made arrow shafts from arrowwood, a thin-stemmed shrub.***

The Mary Gibbs and Jesse H. Jones Reflecting Pool is just one of the many sights in Hermann Park.

Cross a wooden bridge that spans a portion of McGovern Lake. The three-acre lake attracts many birds, including a variety of ducks and black cormorants. Some sections around the lake have been left unmowed to help support wildflowers and wildlife. There are benches and picnic tables here, along with the docking area for rental paddleboats.

Go past the entrance to the Japanese Garden on the left and a large graveled area on the right that has benches and lots of shade. The Mary Gibbs and Jesse H. Jones Reflecting Pool adjoins the resting area. Follow along the reflecting pool to where it ends and turn right.

The statue of Sam Houston can be seen across Hermann Circle Drive. Continue following the trail as it curves right. The Museum of Natural Science is across the street on the left. Follow around the hill that leads to the Miller Outdoor Theatre. Continue on until you return to the reflecting pool. Walk along the eastern edge and, at its head, see the Mecom Fountain, which flows into the pool. At this point, turn left and return to the parking lot.

The Hermann Park Conservancy, working in partnership with the City of Houston, has made world-class improvements to the park.

MILES AND DIRECTIONS

0.0 Start at the wide crushed-granite trail just across the sidewalk from the parking lot at the north entrance and turn right (southwest).

0.1 Pass a sidewalk on the right that leads to Fannin Street and a Metro train platform. Continue straight on the trail.

0.2 Reach a Y and take the left branch. Cross over the tracks for the miniature train.

0.3 Bear left in a semicircle and pass a fenced area on the left, which is the Japanese Garden.

0.5 Continue following the trail and pass over a wooden bridge (GPS: N29 43.909' / W95 23.531'). Turn right (east) at the end of the bridge, then con-

---

🐢 Green Tip:
Observe wildlife from a distance. Do not bend or break off tree branches "to get a better picture." This frightens the wildlife and may destroy part of their camouflage.

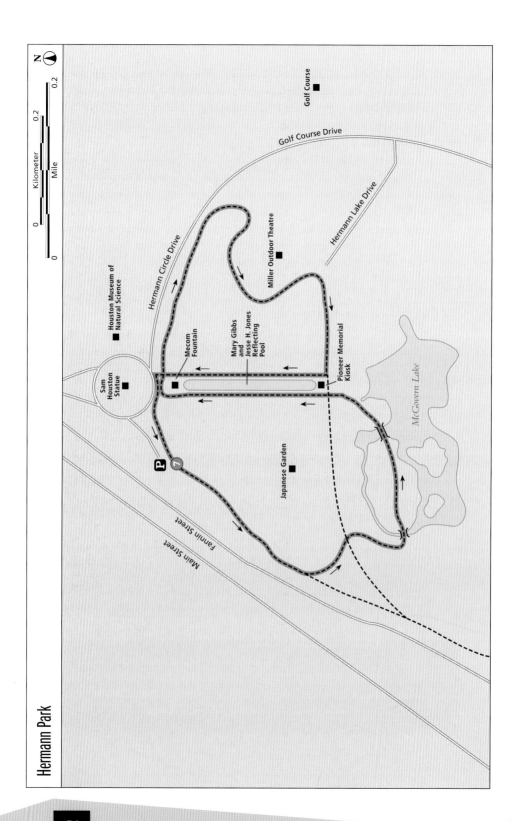

Hermann Park

tinue straight ahead. McGovern Lake is on the right. Continue a short distance and reach another bridge. To the left is a bridge for the children's train. At the end of the bridge, bend left. The paddleboat dock area is on the right.

0.6 Follow the trail left around a small semicircle. Continue north and pass the Pioneer Memorial Kiosk, then turn right and go past the entrance to the Japanese Garden.

0.7 Continue following the trail. The Mary Gibbs and Jesse H. Jones Reflecting Pool is on the right.

0.8 Reach a T where the sidewalk joins the trail. Turn right (east) and follow the trail along Hermann Circle Drive, then bear right into a semicircle and follow the trail. Cross over an area of inlaid bricks, with the water from the Mecom Fountain filling the reflecting pool.

0.9 At this point the Sam Houston statue is directly across Hermann Circle Drive and worth a short out-and-back trip to observe it. Return to the trail and head east.

1.0 Pass a sidewalk to the road on the left. The IMAX Theater (part of the Houston Museum of Natural Science) and skyscrapers can be seen on the left.

1.1 Pass numerous sidewalk paths to the street on the left and on the right a large grassy hill to the Miller Outdoor Theatre. Follow the trail while bearing right.

1.2 Pass a sidewalk on the left that leads to the Miller Theatre. Continue following the trail, bending left around the theater.

1.3 The trail surface changes to brick, with concrete sitting areas on the right and left. Continue following the trail and bearing right.

1.4 Cross a sidewalk and continue straight on the trail. The surface changes back to crushed gravel.

1.5 Reach a T, with the reflecting pool and Japanese Garden straight ahead (GPS: N29 43.120' / W95 23.448'). Take the right branch, heading north. The reflecting pool is adjacent to the left trail edge.

1.7 Reach a T and take the left branch, heading west. Continue following the trail toward the parking area.

1.8 Arrive back at your starting point and proceed to the parking area.

George H. Hermann, Oilman and Philanthropist

George Henry Hermann was born in Houston, Texas, on August 6, 1843, the youngest of four sons of John and Verina (Fannie Mitchell) Hermann. He was named after an older brother, who had died three years earlier. His parents had immigrated from Davos, Switzerland, in 1838, to seek a better life in America.

George inherited his strong work ethic and determination from his parents. With just five dollars cash and some money his mother had received from pawning her jewels, they established one of the first bakeries in Houston. His parents were reasonably successful and expanded their activities to the dairy business.

In the fall of 1861, at the age of eighteen, Hermann joined the 26th Texas Cavalry. He served in the Confederate Army until it was disbanded on May 15, 1865. His father died in 1862 and his mother in 1863, while George was serving the confederacy. After the war, he became involved in the cattle business. In 1872 he became a partner with W. J. and Julius Settegast, and they started selling land as well as cattle. He also operated a sawmill in what is now Hermann Park.

In 1884 Hermann began dealing exclusively in real estate. A few years later he was approached by a person who was 'land poor'—he owned land but didn't have the cash for a horse and buggy that he needed. Hermann was never one to miss an opportunity, so he swapped a team of horses and a buggy for some land in northern Harris County. In 1903 the big Humble oil field was discovered, and the property that he had swapped for was in the center of the field. This made him a multimillionaire. Despite his wealth, he lived frugally and chose to bestow much of his fortune on the people of Houston. He was able to achieve his desire of giving something back to the community.

As the Board of Parks commissioner, Hermann set an example in 1914 by donating 285 acres of land opposite Rice Institute, for the creation of a park. Under the leadership of Houston mayor Ben Campbell, in 1915 the city purchased an additional 122 acres to add to the park. This became Hermann Park, one of Houston's most visited. The Houston Zoo, which opened in 1920, is located within the park. In the spring of 1920, the War Mothers of Houston planted 240 oak trees around the park to honor Harris County soldiers killed in World War I. Some of these trees are still furnishing shade for park visitors. Today the park contains many amenities, including 2 miles of trails (hike 7), a three-acre lake, a children's train ride, and the Theater under the Stars.

After amassing his fortune, Hermann traveled in Europe studying their hospitals and medical facilities. His findings led him to donate ten acres of land in the south end of Houston for the establishment of a charitable hospital. To serve the poor, Hermann Hospital was built and began operating in the area where the Texas Medical Center was later built. When Hermann died in 1914, his will gave the bulk of his estate, valued at $2.6 million, to the city of Houston. The money was to be used for the erection and maintenance of Hermann Hospital.

Hermann made two more notable donations. First he gave a parcel of land to the Houston Art League for the founding of a museum. This became the Museum of Fine Arts and was the first art museum in Texas. The other and possibly the most unique donation was a small park at the site of his childhood home, in front of City Hall. The park was dedicated to his mother, with the stipulation that Houstonians be able to sleep in it overnight, "undisturbed by the forces of law and order." Certainly George Hermann was a philanthropist with a heart. All citizens of Houston—including hikers—continue to benefit from his foresight and generosity.

Edith L. Moore Nature Sanctuary

These short trails are a paradise for bird-watchers and nature lovers. Over 150 species of birds have been seen. Within the park's 17.5 acres, you will cross Rummel Creek and see two oxbows created by the meandering creek. Many bridges and wooden boardwalks add to the hike's interest. This is a great park for families.

Start: Boardwalk behind Edith L. Moore log cabin
Distance: 1.5 miles of interconnecting loops
Approximate hiking time: 1 hour
Difficulty: Easy due to flat, shaded terrain
Trail surface: Mulch, wooden boardwalks
Seasons: Year-round
Other trail users: Bird-watchers
Canine compatibility: Dogs not permitted

Fees and permits: None required; donations accepted
Schedule: Oct–Mar, 7 a.m.–7 p.m.; Apr–Sept, 7 a.m.–9 p.m. Park gates are locked at closing.
Maps: Trail maps available at park office; USGS: Hedwig Village
Trail contact: Houston Audubon Society, 440 Wilchester Blvd., Houston 77079; (713) 932-1639; www.houstonaudubon.org
Other: Restrooms are available at the Edith L. Moore cabin.

Finding the trailhead: From the junction of I-10 West and US 90, go south 11.7 miles on US 90 to exit 756A toward Beltway 8 (West Sam Houston Parkway). In 0.8 mile turn right onto Memorial Drive. In 0.5 mile turn left onto Wilchester Boulevard. Follow Wilchester to the Edith L. Moore Nature Sanctuary at 440 Wilchester Blvd. and turn left into the parking area. The trailhead is located behind the pioneer cabin adjacent to the parking area. Additional parking is available adjacent to the park in the Memorial United Methodist Church west parking area, located at 12955 Memorial Dr. *DeLorme: Texas Atlas & Gazetteer:* Page 128, I5. GPS: N29 46.286' / W95 34.202'

THE HIKE

tart the hike behind the Edith L. Moore log cabin. There are no fewer than 10 named trails, combining to create a hike of 1.5 miles. They loop, interconnect, and join one another through a series of T and Y intersections. Numerous benches are placed strategically along the trails. To add interest to this hike, take along a field guide to birds.

To start the hike, follow a series of boardwalks around a small pond. Cross Rummel Creek on a wooden bridge. This spot offers good photo ops. Take the left branch of the Mary Cravens Trail, heading north-northwest. Follow the loop clockwise. Reach the T intersection with the Creekside Trail and turn left, heading south. Continue on the trail through the woods and near the creek, listening and watching for birds. Depending on the season, great blue herons and great egrets may be seen along the creek. The woods are alive with the singing of numerous species of birds.

The mockingbird is the state bird of Texas. It can mimic over 40 different sounds.

The Edith Moore log cabin is the starting point for the trails in Edith L. Moore Nature Sanctuary. These trails are among the best to view birds year-round.

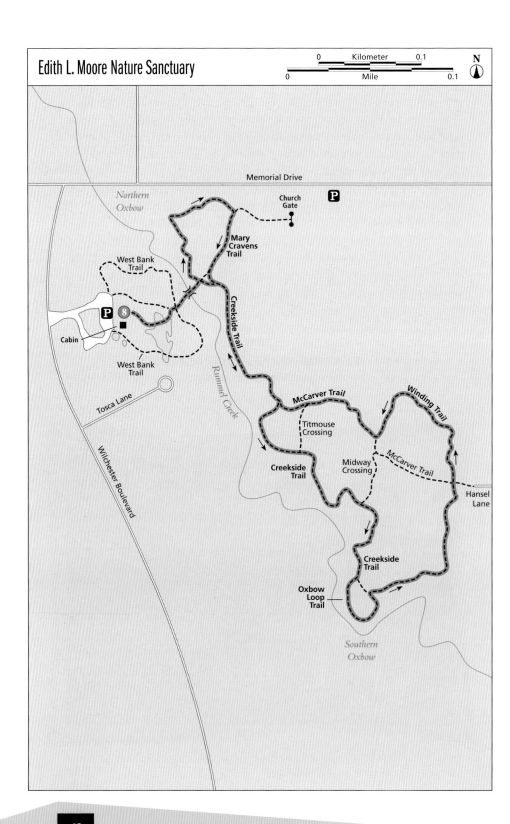

Edith L. Moore Nature Sanctuary

Kilometer
0   0.1

Mile
0   0.1

N

Memorial Drive

Northern Oxbow

Church Gate

P

Mary Cravens Trail

West Bank Trail

P

8

Cabin

West Bank Trail

Creekside Trail

Rummel Creek

Tosca Lane

McCarver Trail

Winding Trail

Titmouse Crossing

Midway Crossing

McCarver Trail

Creekside Trail

Hansel Lane

Witchester Boulevard

Creekside Trail

Oxbow Loop Trail

Southern Oxbow

The trail heads south over some boardwalks and reaches the junction with the McCarver Trail. Follow the right branch, heading west, which is the Creekside Trail. Continue following the trail until nearly reaching Rummel Creek, where the trail makes a hard left and heads south. Listen for the loud drumming of pileated woodpeckers on tree trunks as they look for carpenter ants, a favorite food. This is the largest woodpecker in North America. Continue south, bearing slightly east and away from the creek, then do a semicircle for a short distance, heading north and then bearing right (south) over boardwalks.

The Midway Crossing dead-ends on the left into the Creekside Trail. Stay on the Creekside Trail until you reach the Oxbow Loop on the right (west). Follow the loop around to see the Southern Oxbow created by Rummel Creek. An oxbow is formed when a creek changes direction and leaves behind an isolated section. Rejoin the Creekside Trail and head east and then north. Follow the Creekside Trail north to where it ends and joins the Winding Trail. Continue following the Winding Trail to where it ends and joins the McCarver Trail. Follow McCarver generally west until it intersects Creekside, the longest trail in the sanctuary. Backtrack to the trailhead and log cabin. Unbelievably, all of this happened in less than 1.5 miles.

The sanctuary is maintained by the Houston Audubon Society. Their administrative offices are located on the park grounds.

MILES AND DIRECTIONS

No miles or directions are provided for this hike. The park has numerous short interconnecting trails on 17.5 acres.

> 🌿 **Green Tip:**
> *Stay on marked trails. Veering off the trail can create a new path for water to run off, creating erosion and other problems. Also, walking near the bases of trees can injure their root systems by compacting the soil. Maple trees are especially sensitive.*

Terry Hershey Park: Cardinal and Blue Jay Trails

This hike is for nature enthusiasts and dog walkers, with dog drinking fountains located along the trail. Depending on the season, wildflowers and blooming shrubs line the sides of the bayou, and many species of trees and birds can be seen. Be sure to visit the walk-in sundial, where the shadow you cast shows the time. This lighted path can be enjoyed in the evening.

Start: Cardinal Trail trailhead on north side of parking lot

Distance: 2.2-mile loop

Approximate hiking time: 1.5 hours

Difficulty: Easy due to relatively flat, mostly paved trail

Trail surface: Asphalt, concrete, crushed granite

Seasons: Year-round

Other trail users: Cyclists, in-line skaters, dog walkers

Canine compatibility: Leashed dogs permitted

Fees and permits: None required

Schedule: 7 a.m.–10 p.m.

Maps: Park map available at www .pct3.hctx/parks; USGS: Clodine and Addicks

Trail contact: Harris County Precinct 3 Parks, 3535 War Memorial Dr., Houston 77084; (281) 496-2177

Other: There are no restroom facilities available on the trail.

Finding the trailhead: From the junction of I-10 West and US 90, go 15.8 miles west on I-10. Take exit 753A and drive 0.7 mile to Eldridge Parkway. Follow Eldridge Parkway south for 0.4 mile to Memorial Drive. Turn right onto Memorial Drive. Turn right after 0.3 mile into Terry Hershey Park at 152000 Memorial Dr. *DeLorme: Texas Atlas and Gazetteer:* Page 128, I3. GPS: N29 46.862' / W95 37.467'

THE HIKE

Start on the Cardinal Trail at the trailhead on the north side of the parking lot. A large map on a mounted board is located by the fence just before the park entrance. Near the gate are restrooms and a water fountain. The trail is paved and wheelchair accessible. There is scant tree canopy on the trail to give shade, so be sure to protect yourself with sunscreen and a hat.

Take the connector path by the gazebo to reach the analemmatic sundial—an interesting spot to spend a few minutes. Stand on the month of the year etched in concrete; if the sun is shining, your shadow will be cast across the time of day. Returning to the trail, turn right and head north. Reach a low stone wall and follow the left leg of the loop, heading north toward I-10. Complete the loop, returning to the starting point.

Take the trail left (east) and cross two bridges over South Mayde Creek. There are apartment buildings on the left. Follow the trail as it uses the underpass for Memorial Drive. This section of the hike goes through the park playground and picnic area. The Cardinal Trail ends and the Blue Jay Trail starts. Memorial Mews Street is on the left. An exit from the trail leads to the Molly Pryor Memorial Orchard—an interesting 20-minute side trip. This is a formal orchard, with the trees spaced evenly. The creek continually running alongside the trail adds interest to the hike. Pass some exercise stations and a "runner's shower." At this point South Mayde Creek flows into Buffalo Bayou. Bearing southeast, reach the Eldridge Parkway bridge and cross over the bayou. Going under the bridge to the southeast side leads to the Quail Trail, an out-and-back hike of several miles.

Turn right at the end of the bridge and follow the trail along Buffalo Bayou. The right edge of the trail slopes down to the bayou. The edges are tree and bush covered, ideal habitat for birds. There are a few up-and-down slopes and squiggles to the right and left as the trail heads northwest. Benches are placed strategically along the trail's edge if you need a rest.

Reach a footbridge on the right (northeast). Cross over Buffalo Bayou and continue following the Blue Jay Trail along South Mayde Creek. Depending on the season, this section can have numerous butterflies and birds, including robins, cardinals, and wrens. Many loblolly pines are scattered along the trail's edge, and some earthen mounds have been built on the left of the trail to help hide commercial development. Follow the trail north and under Memorial Drive to arrive back at the parking area.

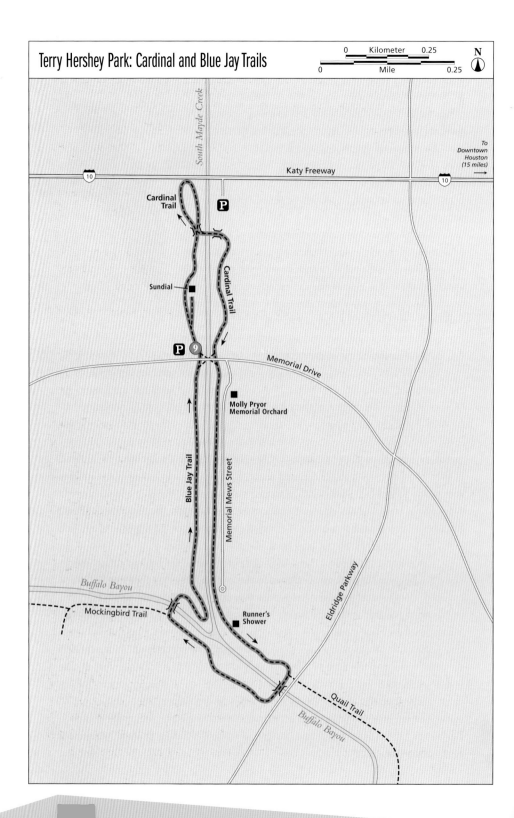

Terry Hershey Park: Cardinal and Blue Jay Trails

0 Kilometer 0.25

0 Mile 0.25

N

Katy Freeway

To Downtown Houston (15 miles) →

10

10

South Mayde Creek

Cardinal Trail

P

Cardinal Trail

Sundial

P 9

Memorial Drive

Molly Pryor Memorial Orchard

Blue Jay Trail

Memorial Mews Street

Eldridge Parkway

Buffalo Bayou

Mockingbird Trail

Runner's Shower

Quail Trail

Buffalo Bayou

0.0 Start at the Cardinal Trail trailhead, just north of the parking lot.

0.1 Take a connector path to reach the analemmatic sundial. Stand on the appropriate stone for the month of the year to show the time of day with your shadow.

0.4 Return to the main trail and follow it northward to a rock-paved resting area with a low wall where the path splits. Take the left (west) path toward I-10.

0.5 Follow the path as it makes a broad turn just before I-10 and return to the rock-paved resting area. Turn left (east) and cross two bridges over South Mayde Creek, then make a hard right, following the path south.

0.8 Use the underpass under Memorial Drive, where the Cardinal Trail ends and the Blue Jay Trail starts.

0.9 Pass a portable toilet on the left (east), a few benches, and some picnic tables with fire grills. South Mayde Creek is on the right (west). Pass an

A young hiker spots a bullfrog along South Mayde Creek, in Hershey Park. Birds and deer may also be seen.

entry gate about 35 feet to the left (east) that leads to Memorial Mews Street and Molly Pryor Memorial Orchard. Continue straight (south) on the paved trail.

1.4 Pass the runner's shower and water fountain on the left (east) and follow the trail, which makes turns toward the left (southeast).

1.5 Pass a bench, where the trail immediately branches. Take the right branch toward Eldridge Parkway. (*Note:* The left branch joins the Quail Trail.) A large signboard with a map of the park shows the trails. At Eldridge Parkway turn right (southwest) and take the pedestrian walkway on the bridge over Buffalo Bayou. Meet the trail on the other side and turn right (northwest).

1.8 Reach a wooden bridge on the right and cross Buffalo Bayou, then follow the trail north.

2.1 A sign on the left (southwest) displays the park rules. At the Y junction bear left (northwest). In about 100 feet go under Memorial Parkway and follow the trail to the parking lot.

2.2 Arrive back at the parking lot.

A Conversation with Terry Hershey

I was fortunate to be able to visit with Terry Hershey during the summer of 2009. She has been a leader in conservation activities at the local, state, and national levels for more than fifty years. For the most part, the awards she has received are too numerous to count, but in 2003 she received the prestigious Pugsley Medal. This is the highest national conservation award given and is bestowed upon only one person each year.

Terry started by telling me of her experiences in 1960 regarding Buffalo Bayou. "The Army Corps of Engineers was straightening and paving the sides of Houston's bayous. I took a group of my neighbors down to where the Corps was working. They had dredged it and were straightening it. The trees and shrubs had all been cut and were being burned along with tires that had been retrieved from the bayou. They would not let the workers take home the lumber to use in heating their homes. It was terrible." She told of speaking with every Houston politician who might be able to help. "Almost without fail they had the same answer: 'They made us do it.' Of course, none of them answered who the all-mighty 'they' was. I gathered a group of friends and we wrote petitions and got 5,000 signatures." Even now as she spoke, the passion was still burning.

She told me she talked with one of the county commissioners, who seemed sympathetic to the cause. "I was on the phone with him, and just as I thought he was getting involved, he abruptly hung up the phone. I realized there would be little to no help from the Houston politicians. They had the 'don't rock the boat' attitude since the federal government was paying for the project."

The Buffalo Bayou Group was formed to help bring more organized pressure. Terry related that George H. W. Bush had recently been elected to the House of Representatives, serving the Houston area, and had been appointed to the powerful Ways and Means Committee. George Mitchell—who would later found and develop The Woodlands, a nationally recognized planned community—lived in the same area as the Hersheys. Terry went on, "I arranged a meeting with the two Georges and let them know what was going on. The straightening and paving of the bayou just seemed exactly the wrong thing to do. They seemed interested." However, they both had some concern over confronting the Army Corps of Engineers.

"It was fortunate that I had gotten to know some of the generals at the Corps through my husband, Jake. He routinely dealt with them on matters concerning his barge company [the largest in the world] on the Mississippi River." Terry said she made many calls to the generals to gather information.

In the interim, Congressman Bush had set up a meeting of the Congressional Appropriations Committee. George Mitchell was supposed to go with him, but at the last minute was unable to attend. Terry was asked to get on the train and attend the meeting. She related events from that meeting: "The chairman of the committee asked, 'Congressman, are you telling us that you don't want to spend money in your district?' There was a small discussion among the committee members and then they left he room. I asked George what was happening. He smiled as he replied, 'I guess we won.'"

This paved the way for the eco-friendly, non-concrete sides of Buffalo Bayou, leaving the bayou with its meandering flow. This, in turn, led to the development of a number of hiking trails along the bayou—a bonanza to the city and to hikers.

Moth caterpillars appear from nowhere to investigate the author's notebook.

John T. Mason Park

Mason Park offers hikers short, tree-filled trails on the east side of Houston. Brays Bayou flows into and then out of the park's 104 acres. The development of 3.5 acres of retention ponds have helped establish a wetland environment for plant and animal life. The bayou and increased wildlife populations add interest to the hike.

Start: Paved trail adjacent to parking lot

Distance: 1.1-mile loop

Approximate hiking time: 45 minutes

Difficulty: Easy due to paved surface and little elevation change

Trail surface: Concrete, asphalt

Seasons: Year-round

Other trail users: Joggers, dog walkers

Canine compatibility: Leashed dogs permitted

Fees and permits: None required

Schedule: Dawn to dusk

Maps: None available in the park; USGS: Park Place

Trail contact: Houston Parks and Recreation Department (HPARD), 2999 South Wayside Dr., Houston 77023; (713) 865-4500; www .houstontx.gov/parks/trails.html

Other: Restroom facilities are in the community center. Water fountains and portable toilets are located near the parking area.

Finding the trailhead: Follow I-45 South toward downtown. Merge onto I-10 East/US 90 East at exit 48A. Stay on I-10 to the McKee Street exit 769C toward Hardy Street and turn right onto McKee Street. Make an easy left onto Runnels Street and then a right onto Navigation Boulevard. After 3.7 miles turn right onto 75th Street. Turn into John T. Mason Park at 541 75th St. The trail is adjacent to the parking area. *DeLorme: Texas Atlas & Gazetteer:* Page 134, A6. GPS: N29 45.702' / W95 22.758'

The trail is adjacent to the parking lot; there is no official trailhead. Use the sidewalk from the parking area and turn right when it Ts into the wide trail. The trail is wheelchair and stroller accessible. Ball fields are on the left. Located on Houston's east side, much of this hike is along Brays Bayou, which enters the park at its northwest corner and then flows across the park in a southeasterly direction.

This wartlike growth is called a burl. It is valuable and used by craftsmen to fashion bowls, expensive pipes, and other goods. This tree is located near the trailhead in John T. Mason Park.

Brays Bayou joins Buffalo Bayou east of the park. Both have miles of what are called linear hike and bike trails, "linear" meaning they are generally out-and-back hikes, bordering the bayou. Many of these can be reached from the Mason Trail. US 90 passes by the west side of the park and brings back the reality of being in the city.

The trail has a number of Y and T branches, but all eventually lead to the section of trail along the bayou and complete the loop back to the parking area. The baseball and soccer fields are clustered near the center of the park.

In 2006 the banks of Brays Bayou were widened to reduce flooding. Three and a half acres were developed as a series of retention ponds, creating a wetland environment. Pass a pond and bear left toward the bayou. The pond may be empty, depending on the amount of recent rainfall. Loblolly pines and southern magnolias are to the left. Go down a slight slope to the bayou. Bald cypress trees have been planted near the water.

Egrets and other shorebirds can be seen flying or standing near the edges of the bayou. Continue walking northwest, with the bayou on the right. Watch for the place where the terrain flattens and is nearly level with the waterway. This is a great spot to do a short out and back to investigate the bayou and its rich assortment of insects and bugs. Depending on the season, wildflowers bloom in this area.

The bayou makes a lazy bend left and then right as it flows under the 75th Street bridge. Turn left (south) at the 75th Street bridge and continue on the sidewalk to the parking area.

In 1930 Dora Porter Mason donated 69.88 acres in memory of her husband, John. The city combined this with other parcels to create a 104-acre park and named it in honor of John T. Mason.

MILES AND DIRECTIONS

0.0 Start at the trailhead that adjoins the parking lot and is located near the Spanish mission–style community center building. Turn right and follow the concrete trail south.

0.1 Reach a Y and take the right branch, heading southeast.

0.2 The asphalt trail changes to concrete just before reaching a Y. Take the right branch and follow the trail east.

0.3 Pass a retaining pond on the left and reach a Y. Take the left branch, heading north. Brays Bayou can be seen straight ahead.

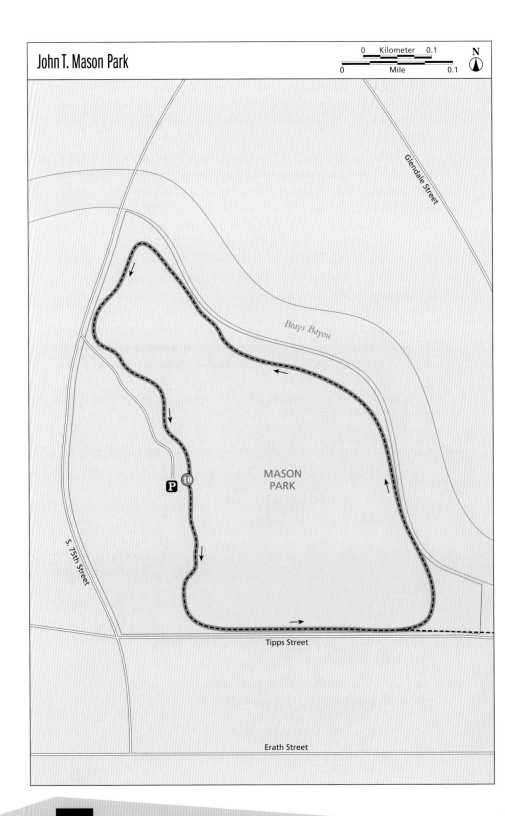

John T. Mason Park

0   Kilometer   0.1

0   Mile   0.1

N

Glendale Street

Brays Bayou

MASON PARK

P ⑩

S. 75th Street

Tipps Street

Erath Street

0.4 Reach a T, with the bayou directly ahead. Take the left and follow the trail along the bayou (GPS: N29 43.482′ / W95 17.525′).

0.5 Reach a Y. Take the left branch, following alongside the bayou. This is a good spot to go down to the edge of the bayou and then return to the trail.

0.6 Bear to the left (north/northwest) as the bayou bends to the right and continues toward the 75th Street bridge.

0.7 A narrow dirt bike path joins the trail from the left. Continue following the paved trail northwest. Pass several concrete picnic tables and benches on the left.

0.8 Take a sharp left away from the bayou and along 75th Street.

0.9 Turn left at the park entrance gate, heading southeast onto the asphalt trail toward the parking area.

1.1 Follow the trail until you reach the trailhead. End the hike and return to the parking lot.

The white ash tree is called the "baseball bat tree" due to its tough and elastic wood, which is excellent to use for baseball bats.

11

Keith-Weiss Park

It's always great to find a new trail. This paved trail around the flood-control retention ponds was opened in August 2008 and takes advantage of both the forest and the ponds. An area was cleared for the ponds in this 500-acre park's forest, and the fish and birds moved in quickly. A curving boardwalk with observation platforms and benches crosses the main pond and provides many good photo ops.

Start: Sidewalk trail adjacent to northeast side of parking area
Distance: 2.3-mile lollipop
Approximate hiking time: 1.5 hours
Difficulty: Easy due to paved trail with little up and down
Trail surface: Concrete sidewalks
Seasons: Year-round
Other trail users: Dog walkers, cyclists, bird-watchers
Canine compatibility: Leashed dogs permitted

Fees and permits: None required
Schedule: Dawn to dusk
Maps: Park maps available at www.houstontx.gov/parks/trails .html; USGS: Humble
Trail contact: Houston Parks and Recreation Department (HPARD), 2999 South Wayside Dr., Houston 77023; (713) 865-4500; www .houstontx.gov/parks/trails.html
Other: A portable toilet is located in the parking area. Scooters and skateboards are prohibited.

Finding the trailhead: From I-10 East take exit 768A on the left to merge onto I-45 toward Dallas. Follow I-45 to exit 51 and merge onto I-610 East. Take exit 19B off I-610 East for the Hardy Toll Road North (TX 548). In 3 miles exit the Hardy Toll Road at the Little York Road exit. Follow Little York Road and turn left onto Aldine West-field Road. Follow Aldine Westfield for 1.3 miles, past Mierianne Street, and turn into Keith-Weiss Park at the parking area. *DeLorme: Texas Atlas & Gazetteer:* Page 130, A3. GPS: N29 53.397' / W95 21.285'

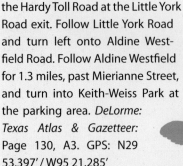

THE HIKE

Start the trail, which is all on concrete sidewalks with a few minor up-and-down grades, from the northeast side of the parking area. The sidewalks are just inside the park gate. Take the right branch of the trail, heading away from the soccer fields. Two pavilions and a playground are on the left. Follow the trail as it veers left past the tennis courts. At about 0.25 mile leave the playground/ball

These young hikers investigate a turtle near a retaining pond in Keith-Weiss Park.

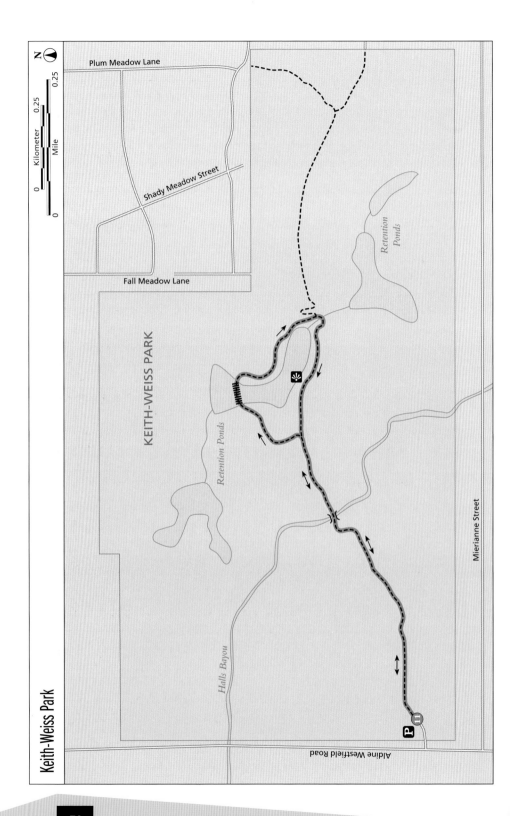

Keith-Weiss Park

field area and enter the woods. The woods are mostly hardwoods, including live oaks, with a few large loblolly pines. The trail is cleared for about 15 feet to the woods on each side.

The bridge that crosses Halls Bayou provides an opportunity to inspect the bayou, which bisects the park. Shorebirds may be seen along the edges of the bayou. The trail alternates between partial and no tree canopy, so wear a hat and sunscreen. Birds may be heard in the woods, including the distinct notes of the song sparrow. Listen for three or four notes followed by a *tow-wee*. There are some interesting stone blocks along the trail, some of them large enough to sit on.

As you approach the retention ponds, you'll notice that the terrain has been altered by bulldozers. The forest has been cleared and the land shaped to slope down gently to the basins. The landscaping expertly blends the ponds with the surrounding forest. Birds and other water-loving creatures have made the ponds their home, and bird-watchers are already considering this a premier location.

The hike follows around and across the ponds. A long wooden boardwalk winds its way over the largest pond. There are several observation areas on the boardwalk, with benches and informational signs. Depending on the season, hundreds of birds can be seen in or around the pond, including egrets, herons, and ducks.

A smaller pond joins the larger pond via an overflow ditch. Follow the trail going between the ponds. Pass a wooden observation deck at the edge of the pond on the right. Continue following the trail, going away from the ponds until you reach an inverted Y. There are two large orange rectangular stones at this point. Take the left branch and backtrack to the trailhead.

This 500-acre park in the middle of a forest on the city's northeast side holds great promise to hikers, as more trails are planned.

MILES AND DIRECTIONS

0.0 Start at the trailhead (concrete sidewalk) at the northeast corner of the parking area.

0.2 Reach a T intersection and take the right (east) branch. Pass tennis courts on the right and head into a wooded area.

0.3 Bear right, following the trail, and pass an incoming sidewalk on the left (north).

0.4 Follow the trail as it bends left and right then goes straight.

0.5 Cross over a culvert and then a bridge that crosses Halls Bayou. Cross over another culvert shortly after the end of the bridge.

0.7   Pass some rock slabs on the right and left, large enough to sit on, and reach a Y intersection. Take the left (north) branch and continue following the trail.

0.8   Pass a bench on the left and an information sign on the right that tells about helping nature make stormwater cleaner.

0.9   Continue toward the retention ponds and bear slightly left (north). Then head right (east) and reach the boardwalk that crosses the pond.

1.0   After crossing the pond, curve right and head south. The retention pond is on the right. Follow the trail and bend slightly left (east), following around the pond edge.

1.2   Bear slightly left (east) and pass a stone retaining wall at the end of the pond.

1.3   Follow the trail around the pond and reach a T intersection. Take the right branch and cross an overflow ditch from another pond. The main retaining pond is on the right.

1.4   Go past an observation deck on the right, at the edge of the pond. Continue mostly straight with a little jog here and there. The main pond is to the right.

1.6   Pass two large orange rectangular stones and reach an inverted Y junction. Take the branch to the left (straight) and backtrack to the trailhead.

2.3   Arrive back at the trailhead and return to the parking area.

Journaling—More Fun on the Trail

If you're not hiking with some specific purpose other than to simply enjoy the outdoors, journaling can be a great way to add a new dimension to a family or social hike. A friend of mine had recently given me some instructions on trail observation and how to keep a trail journal. Prior to that I wasn't sure what journaling was. Like the words yodeling and pedaling, it sounded interesting and as though it involved action, but I didn't know exactly what it involved and how it fit in with hiking.

My friend explained that journaling is simply keeping a rough set of notes on what you observe on or near the trail. You don't need to be a writer or scientist. The most interesting aspect is the methods of observation. These include closing your eyes and listening, scooping up some dirt to feel, and covering your ears and watching. The idea is to use all of your senses to enhance the experience.

The minimum items needed to start a journal are something to write with and something to write on. Some general rules on how to start the journal: In the upper right-hand corner of the page, record the date, time, location, weather, and habitat for each hike. This gives a reference point for future use of the notes. Each hiker records the things that are of interest to him or

her, including drawings. Some folks, like me, have difficulty drawing a stick man, but give it a try—maybe start out with a dandelion.

I decided to try out some of the techniques, which sounded like a great inexpensive family activity. I asked my daughter Kim, her 14-year-old son Nate, and Kim's mother, Kay, to accompany me. Kim wasn't sure what I was trying to accomplish. I convinced her that hiking and journaling would give her a chance to slow down and focus on something other than work. Nate led the way to the trail that paralleled a road. A 5-minute limit was set to walk about 75 yards up the trail at a normal pace, and 15 minutes to return while using our new observation skills. At the end of the 75-yard walk, and to our amazement, there wasn't much difference in any of the journals. All of us had seen trees, bushes, and sky. Nate had seen a couple of worms and a low-flying bee, while Kim noticed a salamander that Kay and I had not recorded.

It was now time to start back and make more observations. We stopped every 10 to 15 yards to listen, watch, touch, smell, and possibly taste. Nate was the only one to actually taste something, taking some blooms from a honeysuckle bush and showing us they were edible. At each stop we looked straight ahead and then stooped, stood up, covered our eyes and listened, and then covered our ears and watched. What we saw and heard became entries in our journals, and included wind rustling, birds chirping, people, the path, ants, a squirrel climbing a tree, sky with clouds, pine needles and cones, small and large bushes, red flowers, poison ivy, a hole in a tree, a turkey vulture circling in the sky, and pine and hardwood trees.

Things had been felt that were hard, soft, slippery, waxy, coarse, smooth, dry, and wet. Colors noted were green, yellow, brown, black, and white and a rainbow-colored leaf. After discovering something new, we were often surprised at how many times we continued to see it, and realized that we must have walked past it many times before without noticing it. The return trip almost became a game. The writing stopped being a task and became a fun part of our trip.

Back home, we were all excited about the hike. From our enthusiasm, there was no doubt that journaling had added an interesting dimension to the trip. Try it—you could like it.

Herman Brown Park

This 750-acre park on the northeast edge of the city is an oasis for hikers. Even though the park is surrounded by residential communities, its trails pass through bottomland hardwood forest containing live oak, black willow, and cypress. Hunting Bayou adds interest as it bisects the park. The bayou also attracts neotropical birds as they stop on their migration flights.

Start: Asphalt maintenance road on east side of parking area
Distance: 2.8-mile loop with a short out and back
Approximate hiking time: 1.5 hours
Difficulty: Easy due to paved flat trails
Trail surface: Asphalt, crushed granite, mulch
Seasons: Year-round
Other trail users: Dog walkers

Canine compatibility: Leashed dogs permitted
Fees and permits: None required
Schedule: 5 a.m.–10 p.m.
Maps: Park maps available at www.houstontx.gov/parks/trails.html; USGS: Jacinto City
Trail contact: Houston Parks and Recreation Department (HPARD), 2999 South Wayside Dr., Houston 77023; (713) 845-1000; www.houstontx.gov/parks/trails.html

Finding the trailhead: From the junction of I-10 East and US 59, follow I-10 for 5.6 miles to exit 776A toward Mercury Drive. After 0.1 mile bear slightly left onto East Freeway. In 0.2 mile turn left onto Mercury Drive. Continue straight and turn into Herman Brown Park at 400 Mercury Dr., northeast of the I-10 and I-610 interchange. The trailhead is located at the end of the parking area. *DeLorme: Texas Atlas & Gazetteer:* Page 131, H8.
GPS: N29 46.955' / W95 14.739'

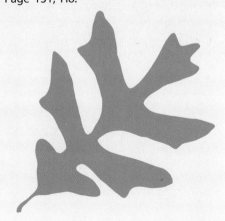

THE HIKE

Start the hike from the east side of the parking area, just past the gate at the asphalt maintenance road. Turn right, heading east. There are lights on the left side, allowing some hiking after dusk. Due to Hurricane Ike in September 2008 and extensive road construction on I-610 that divided the park, the former trail names are no longer applicable.

Pass a few picnic tables on the right and then cross a short wooden bridge over a shallow gully. Reach the Brown Pavilion, which has water fountains and restrooms. Two tennis courts are on the left, and the area is lighted. There are stone trail marker posts at the intersection of most trails. They are mainly used to identify points of interest, such as the lake, the bayou overlook, and the direction to the Brown Pavilion and to the soccer/baseball fields.

Turn left onto a gravel trail that leads to a very small lake; the path follows around the lake, which is stocked with rainbow trout during January and February by the Texas Parks & Wildlife Department. It is probably best to avoid the elbow-to-elbow crowds of anglers during these periods. The area around the lake can be swampy, depending on the amount of rainfall. Backtrack from the lake to the main trail and resume the hike from the turnoff.

Continue following the trail and signs to reach the Hunting Bayou overlook. Pass live oaks, willows, cypress trees, and a few loblolly pines, with a scattering of palmettos as part of the forest understory. In any season of the year, birds can be heard singing in the woods. A stone marker identifies the wooden platform, which is situated about 30 feet above the bayou. The bayou forms a lazy S as it flows from north to south. Hunting Bayou is a tributary of Buffalo Bayou, and both are magnets for migrating birds. Great blue herons and white egrets are among the birds commonly seen at the water's edge.

Backtrack to the main trail. Continue following the main trail, which has heavy forest on both sides. The trail turns right and left but generally heads west toward I-610 and then back south toward the Brown Pavilion. Cross a small wooden bridge over a shallow creek.

Follow the trail back to the junction near the Brown Pavilion and backtrack to the trailhead and parking area.

🌿 Green Tip:
When your dog is off leash, do not allow Fido to chase wildlife or disturb birds by barking at them. Most wildlife will move when they realize loose dogs are in their territory. Be considerate.

0.0 Start at the trailhead adjacent to the east side of the parking area at the gate barring access to the asphalt maintenance road. Turn right onto the maintenance road and head straight (east).

0.1 Pass a picnic table and a path on the right (south) that makes a small loop and rejoins the trail.

0.2 Pass several picnic tables and a path on the right that dead-ends into the trail. Continue straight and cross a short bridge over a gully. In about 200 yards, pass a gate blocking the trail. The Brown Pavilion is ahead on the right and tennis courts are on the left. There are water fountains and restrooms at the pavilion. Continue straight on a narrow crushed-granite trail.

The pond along the trail in Herman Brown Park offers interesting reflections on sunny days and shoulder-to-shoulder anglers during trout season.

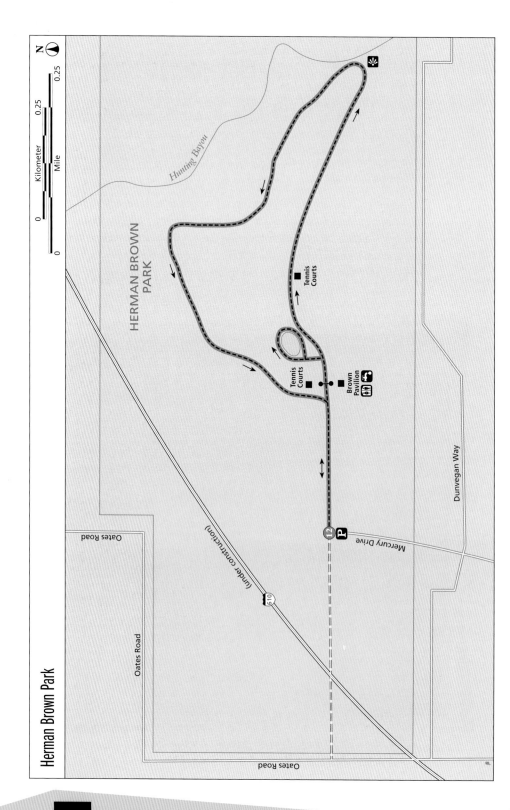

Herman Brown Park

0.3 Intersect with a trail. Turn left, heading north toward a very small lake. Reach the lake and walk the loop trail around it.

0.4 Follow around the lake and return to the point where the lake loop started. Backtrack to the trail junction.

0.5 After backtracking, reach a stone trail marker on the left and tennis court on the right. Turn left, heading east on the asphalt trail.

0.6 Continue straight on the trail and then make a hard left, heading north at a bench on the right side.

0.8 Reach a Y intersection and take the right branch, heading east. There is a bench and stone trail maker.

1.1 Turn left onto an asphalt trail. Head north for 0.1 mile and then make a hard right, heading southeast.

1.2 Reach a trail marker and make a hard left, heading northeast to the bayou overlook.

1.3 Reach the bayou overlook platform. Hunting Bayou lies below the platform to the northeast. Follow the trail from the overlook, heading northwest.

1.7 Continue following the trail northwest until you reach a bridge. Pass the bridge and bear slightly to the right, heading north.

1.9 Follow the trail and take a hard left, heading west.

2.2 Take a hard left onto a path, heading south.

2.3 Cross a bridge and follow the trail to the right, heading west.

2.6 Follow the trail, making a hard left turn and heading south. In less than 0.1 mile reach the T intersection with the asphalt maintenance road near the Brown Pavilion. Take the right branch, heading west to the trailhead.

2.8 Arrive back at the trailhead.

The monarch butterfly is the most watched and tracked insect in North America. It is the only insect to perform a migration that spans the continent. Its flight through central Texas reaches its peak in early October.

Bear Creek Nature Trail

Hike over an area that had been farmed by German immigrants and their descendants for one hundred years. At Bear Creek Pioneers Park, deer are common and frogs and empty snail shells are numerous. Venomous snakes (water moccasins and copperheads) as well as several species of nonvenomous snakes may be seen in late spring through early fall. This is a pleasant hike through a forest of hardwood trees. Enjoy being in the woods and exploring nature.

Start: Bear Creek Nature Trail trailhead, about 500 feet south of equestrian parking area
Distance: 3.6-mile loop
Approximate hiking time: 2 hours
Difficulty: Moderate due to some swampy sections and length of trail
Trail surface: Bark mulch, dirt
Seasons: Year-round
Other trail users: Equestrians for a short distance

Canine compatibility: Dogs not permitted
Fees and permits: None required
Schedule: 7 a.m.–dusk
Maps: None available in the park; park map available at www .pct3.hctx.net/parks/bearcreek pioneers.aspx; USGS: Addicks
Trail contact: Harris County Precinct 3 Parks, 3535 War Memorial Dr., Houston 77084; (281) 496-2177

Finding the trailhead: From the junction of I-10 West/US 90, go 15.8 miles west. Take exit 753A toward Eldridge Parkway. Turn right onto North Eldridge Parkway and follow the parkway 2.8 miles. Turn left onto War Memorial Drive and in 0.2 mile turn into Bear Creek Road at 3535 War Memorial Dr. The trailhead and parking are at the Equestrian Trail parking area. *DeLorme: Texas Atlas & Gazetteer:* Page 128, E2. GPS: N29 49.391'/ W95 38.044'

THE HIKE

Start at the trailhead located through a meadow, about 500 feet south of the equestrian parking area. Take the right branch, heading east, and within 100 yards turn south and enter heavy woods. This loop is often very close to the Equestrian Trail, so horses may be present. The trail has little to no signage, so keep track of your location.

Bear right and then follow the trail straight. Heavy woods, including large oaks, maples, and cedar elms, line the trail. Some of the trees have long strands of Spanish moss hanging from them. The woods contain many trees that were downed by Hurricane Ike in September 2008. They will be left to decay naturally and furnish nutrients to the forest. One of the uprooted trees along the trail's edge is a water oak. Ironically, the trail-edge sign identifying it is still standing. There are no benches, but it's easy to find a log to rest on.

The trail makes a number of turns to the right and left. Just ahead of a Y at 0.3 mile, pass a sign on the right stating NATURE TRAIL. Take the left branch, heading east. Pass through a swampy area where deer tracks are numerous. Try to guess the size of the deer by the size of the track. There are clumps of maidenhair ferns, some 6 feet tall. The trail through the woods gives a constantly changing picture as the seasons change. Any season is a good time to hear birds singing in the trees. Cardinals are especially easy to spot due to their red feathers. The trail meanders left and right and sometimes makes a semicircle. While in the swampy area, watch and listen for toads and frogs. Large empty snail shells are scattered about. Please leave these for others to enjoy. Continue following the loop counterclockwise back to the trailhead.

Bear Creek Pioneers Park is located on the Addicks Reservoir. The reservoir was created in the 1940s by the U.S. Army Corps of Engineers to help prevent a reoccurrence of the catastrophic flooding that hit Houston in 1935. Bear Creek, for which the park is named, flows through the park and is one of the major tributaries of Buffalo Bayou. This area is a fertile hiking region, with George Bush Park, Edith L. Moore Nature Sanctuary, Terry Hershey Park, Westside Hike and Bike Trail, and Boone Road Park all close by.

MILES AND DIRECTIONS

Note: GPS points have been included to assist in navigating through dense woods with no signage and parts of the trail that have been blocked by trees downed by Hurricane Ike.

0.0   Start at the trailhead on the right at the south end of the parking lot.

0.1   Follow the trail east and immediately go into the woods.

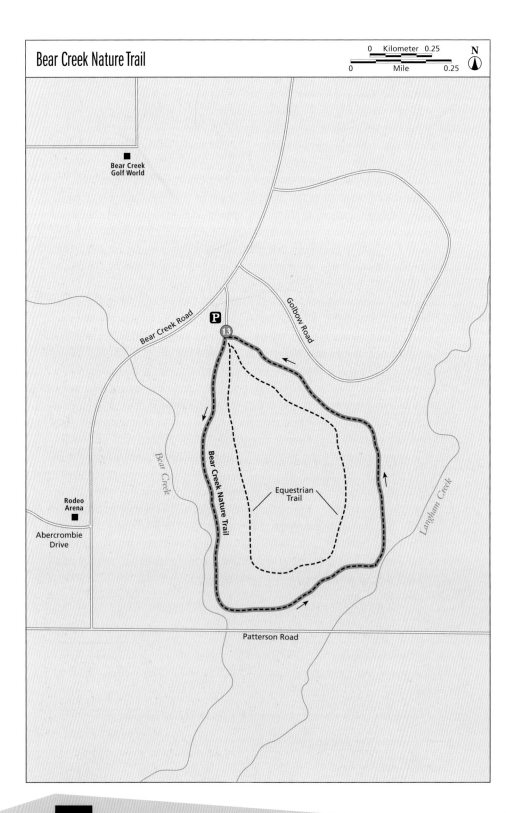

Bear Creek Nature Trail

Bear Creek Golf World

Bear Creek Road

Golbow Road

P

13

Bear Creek

Bear Creek Nature Trail

Equestrian Trail

Langham Creek

Rodeo Arena

Abercrombie Drive

Patterson Road

0   Kilometer   0.25
0   Mile   0.25

N

0.2 Follow the trail, bearing left and then right, heading south. Pass clumps of ferns and a nature trail sign on the right.

0.3 Reach a Y and take the left branch, which leads through a clearing.

0.5 Follow the trail through a series of left and right meanderings. Reach an uprooted tree on the right, marked by a sign that says WATER OAK (GPS: N29 49.178′ / W95 38.135′). Bear left (southeast) at the sign and follow the trail past ferns on the right and left.

The swampy areas near the Bear Creek Nature Trail offer the opportunity to see snails and other critters, including deer and water snakes.

0.6   Reach a sign reading CEDAR ELM, on the right (GPS: N29 49.178'/ W95 38.135'). Bear left at the sign, then continue in an arc to the left (east) and follow the trail south.

0.7   Follow the trail as it zigzags.

0.9   Cross over a drain tile running under the trail.

1.0   Bear slightly right (southwest) through a swampy area. The trail continues to bend left and right.

1.2   Reach a signpost on the right that says NATURE TRAIL (GPS: N29 48.875' / W95 38.058').

1.3   Pass very large loblolly pine (more than 3 feet in diameter and 80 feet tall) on the right at the trail's edge.

1.5   Go through a possibly swampy area (depending on when it rained), bearing left and then following the trail in a semicircle to the left.

1.6   Follow the trail and bear hard right (east) (GPS: N29 48.902' / W95 37.887').

1.9   Follow the trail, making a hard left (northeast) and an immediate right (east).

2.1   Follow the trail past some very large trees that were uprooted by Hurricane Ike. The trail continues to meander left and right.

2.6   Continue straight on the trail and then take a hard right (GPS N29 49.148'/ W95 37.575').

2.8   The trail bears left and then follows a short semicircular route.

3.1   The trail zigzags and goes straight. Make a hard right (north) and then proceed west (GPS: N29 49.277' / W95 37.840').

3.5   Reach a Y. Take the left (north) branch and then bend to the right. Pass a sign on the left, tacked about 7 feet high in a tree, that says START TALL PINE TRAIL (GPS: N29 49.277' / W95 37.840'). Head into the meadow on the right and walk about 50 yards.

3.6   Arrive back at the trailhead.

Lake Houston Wilderness Park: Hoot Owl and Magnolia Trails

This wilderness park is true to its name with heavy woods plus two creeks. The habitat provides an ideal home to birds, mammals, insects, and snakes. The opportunity to hear the songs of many bird species and observe the tracks of deer, armadillos, raccoons, and other mammals is excellent. Butterflies, dragonflies, and mosquitoes are also present. Many wooden bridges aid in crossing gullies and streams. The nature lover, bird-watcher, or solitude seeker will enjoy this trail. This hike is suitable for families with young children.

Start: Hoot Owl Trail trailhead, southwest of park headquarters

Distance: 1.7 miles out and back with a small loop

Approximate hiking time: 1.5 hours

Difficulty: Easy due to flat trails and good shade

Trail surface: Dirt, sand

Seasons: Year-round

Other trail users: Dog walkers, bird-watchers

Canine compatibility: Leashed dogs permitted

Fees and permits: Small entrance fee per person age 13–65

Schedule: Gate open 8 a.m.–8 p.m. Sun–Thurs, 8 a.m.–10 p.m. Fri–Sat. Office hours 8 a.m.–5 p.m. every day.

Maps: Trail maps available at the park office; USGS: Moonshine Hill, Splendora

Trail contact: Park Manager, 22031 Baptist Encampment Rd., New Caney 77357; (281) 354-6881; Houston Parks and Recreation Department (HPARD), 2999 South Wayside Dr., Houston 77023; (713) 865-4500; www.houstontx.gov/parks/trails.html

Other: Potable water at park office and nature center. Restrooms at nature center and near the trestle bridge. Pets are not allowed in buildings. This is the only City of Houston park that offers camping facilities. The park is a game preserve.

Finding the trailhead: From downtown Houston take I-45 North to the exit for Beltway 8 East. Merge onto Beltway 8 East and proceed 5.8 miles east, then merge onto US 59 North, toward Cleveland. Follow US 59 North for 16 miles and then take the TX 1485/New Caney exit. After 0.5 mile turn right onto FM 1485 East. After 1.9 miles turn right onto Baptist Encampment Road and follow the Lake Houston Park signs for 1.6 miles to the park entrance at 22031 Baptist Encampment Rd. Follow the park road for about 1 mile to the paved parking area near the park headquarters. *DeLorme: Texas Atlas & Gazetteer:* Page 72, G1. GPS: N30 8.312' / W95 10.364'

THE HIKE

Start at the park headquarters. Sign in, pay the entrance fee, and get a trail map and Magnolia Interpretive Trail brochure. Head south to the Hoot Owl Trail trailhead opposite the parking area. The trail crosses over a gravel path with 4-by-4s lining its edges. Follow Hoot Owl, which is 4 feet wide with a dirt surface, into the woods.

In 100 yards reach the first of five wooden footbridges. After crossing the bridge, which spans a gully 5 feet below, bear right and then hard right, temporarily heading east. Heavy woods are on the left and a dry creek gully is on the right. Bear left, heading away from the gully, and reach the second bridge. Cross the bridge and, after going up the steps at the end, immediately bear right. Pass a bench on the right and take a hard right, continuing to follow the trail. Heavy woods containing magnolias, oaks, and sugarberry are on the right and left, and the terrain is generally flat. A good tree canopy furnishes shade but allows the sun to trickle through and create interesting patterns. Watch for wispy spider webs in the spring and fall. Squirrels are numerous and can be seen chasing each other, or gathering nuts in the fall. A few large loblolly pines act as sentinels along the edge of the trail.

After hiking about 0.25 mile and zigzagging right and left, go down a slight slope to reach the third bridge, about 20 feet in length. This seasonal creek bed and surrounding gully meander back and forth across the trail. Pass a sign on the left identifying the Hoot Owl Trail that you're on. Continue a short distance and pass a path intersecting from the right and leading to Camp Magnolia. Follow Hoot Owl as it squiggles from the right to the left and back, and watch for insects and small lizards on the ground. Pass a trail sign on the right pointing to Camp Ironwood and Camp Magnolia. Reach a T and take the left (southwest) branch, going by a large two-trunked magnolia tree. Follow the trail for 100 yards and reach a 40-foot-long wooden bridge. The bridge crosses Joe's Creek, an intermittent stream that has water after a rain. Joe's Creek forms part of a ravine ecosystem, and its water eventually flows into Peach Creek.

The ravine's moist nature attracts many animals and plants. This is excellent habitat for the Carolina wren, which nests year-round in the underbrush. Watch for this small bird with a deep rust-brown head and back and an orange-yellow chest. The easiest thing to spot is its prominent white eye stripe. Its song, a melodious TEAKETTLE TEA-TEAKETTLE TEA, may be heard any time of the day.

Follow the trail for 200 feet, passing some large magnolia trees and loblolly pines until reaching a Y. There is a wooden bench on the right. Take the right branch, heading west. Pass marker 14 as the trail heads down to Peach Creek. Use caution, as this area can be slippery when wet. At the creek edge, turn right and follow the path to the scenic rest stop. There is a bench here that overlooks the creek, which is shallow with a gravelly bottom. The sandbars in the creek create a good photo op. Return to the trail and follow it along the creek, which is on the right. This is a good place to look in the sand for animal tracks.

Follow the trail with the creek on the right, then bear hard left and away from the creek as the trail loops back to the Magnolia Interpretive Trail. The trail wanders to the left and right as it passes markers 7 through 12. Pass a sign for the Peach

A father tells his sons how rotting branches return energy to the soil and furnish a home for ants, lichens, and other organisms.

Lake Houston Wilderness Park: Hoot Owl and Magnolia Trails

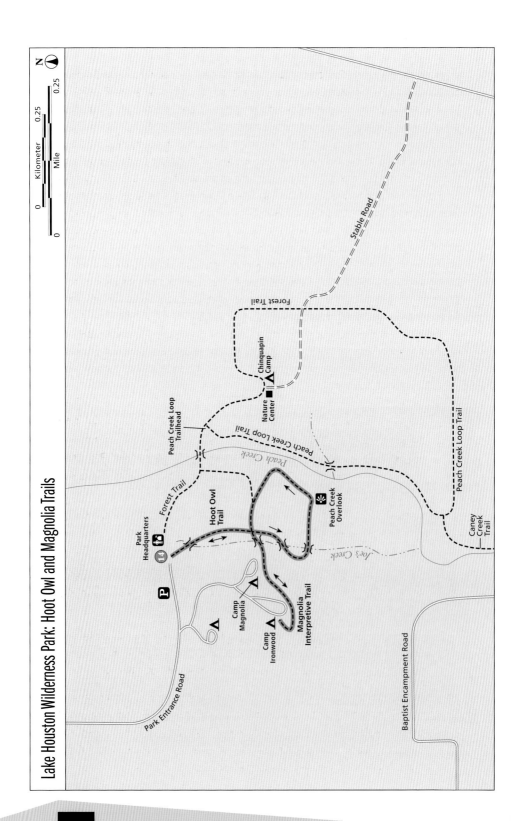

Creek Wildlife Tracking Trail and go up a slight slope to a T with the Magnolia Interpretive Trail. Take the left branch, passing some trees downed by Hurricane Ike in 2008. The left edge of the trail slopes down to a 20-foot-wide gully, while the right edge borders the woods.

Complete the loop back at markers 16 and 17 and a T branch. Take the right branch and backtrack past Joe's Creek Bridge. Continue 200 feet to a Y. Stop backtracking and take the left branch, heading southwest. The trail is flat, with a few slopes up and down. Cross a 20-foot-long wooden bridge—this is number five. Head left at the end of the bridge, with heavy woods on both the right and left. Watch for deer and small mammal tracks while passing markers 21 through 25. At 1 mile into the trail, reach a Y and take the left branch, heading to Camp Ironwood. Benches, tables, and grills are available at the camp, which is located in the woods. This is a great place to rest and contemplate the hike. The Magnolia Interpretive Trail trailhead is at Camp Ironwood. Backtrack to the Y and take the right branch onto Hoot Owl Trail. Follow Hoot Owl Trail to the trailhead and end the hike.

The park has plans over the next five years to change the entrance roadway and to add several miles of new trails.

MILES AND DIRECTIONS

0.0 Start from the Hoot Owl Trail trailhead southwest of the park headquarters. Head east and almost immediately cross a gravel trail with 4-by-4 timbers bordering each side. Within 100 yards, cross a wooden footbridge over a gully about 5 feet below the bridge. Bear left (north), with the gully about 6 feet away.

0.1 Reach another wooden bridge with six steps going up at its end. Immediately bear right, heading southwest. Follow the trail about 100 yards and pass a wooden bench on the right.

0.2 Follow the Hoot Owl Trail, bearing right. Go down a slight slope and reach a 20-foot-long wooden bridge. Cross the bridge and pass a trail marker that shows Hoot Owl as continuing straight ahead.

0.3 Pass a trail that intersects from the right and leads to Camp Magnolia. Continue on the Hoot Owl Trail as it winds right and left through the woods for about 100 yards to a T. Take the left branch, heading southwest.

0.4 Go down a slight slope to a wooden footbridge. Cross over the bridge, which is about 40 feet long; at the end of the bridge is a sign that reads JOE'S CREEK—an intermittent creek. Follow the trail for 200 feet and reach a Y. There is a wooden bench on the right and six benches on the left, forming an outdoor classroom. Take the right branch, heading east.

0.5 Pass Magnolia Interpretive Trail marker 14 and continue down a slope to the edge of Peach Creek. Follow a path on the right to reach the scenic rest stop. A bench is provided that overlooks the creek. Return to the trail and bear left, following the creek. Pass marker 12 on the right.

0.6 Follow the trail, bearing hard left away from the creek. Pass markers 11, 10, 9, 8, and 7 on the right.

0.7 Bear left and pass marker 6 on the left and then bear right and pass a sign that says PEACH CREEK WILDLIFE TRACKING TRAIL. Go up a slight slope and reach a T with the Magnolia Interpretive Trail. Take the left branch, heading east.

0.8 Continue following the Magnolia Interpretive Trail as it loops by markers 16 and 17. At the T take the right branch near marker 17 and backtrack to Joe's Creek Bridge.

0.9 Continue following the trail while backtracking until reaching a Y. Take the left branch, heading southwest, then go down a slight slope and immediately cross a wooden bridge. Pass marker 20 at the end of the bridge.

1.0 Continue following the trail, heading generally south, and pass marker 21 on the left, then 22, 23, 24, and 25 on the right. Reach marker 26 and the Camp Ironwood sign on the right, then almost immediately reach a Y and take the left branch.

1.1 Follow the trail as it leads into a small clearing about 80 feet long, with marker 27 on the left. Bear right at the end of the clearing and reach Camp Ironwood. Backtrack on the Magnolia Interpretive Trail to the Y where it meets Hoot Owl Trail.

1.2 Continue backtracking and pass markers 25, 24, 23, 22, 21, and 20 and cross over the bridge.

1.4 Continue following the trail and pass Camp Magnolia. Reach a Y and take the right branch, heading north onto the Hoot Owl Trail toward the trailhead.

1.7 End the hike at the Hoot Owl trailhead.

Animal Tracks

Observing and attempting to identify animal tracks can add an extra dimension to a hike. Tracks are usually more prevalent near creeks and ponds, where the critters go for water. The most common mammal tracks to look for on the trails near Houston are white-tailed deer, domestic dog, raccoon, squirrel, opossum, armadillo, and skunk. For some of these animals, seeing their tracks may be as close as you get to them.

The distinctive white-tailed deer track is among the easiest to find. Their prints are usually clear and large, 2 to 4 inches in length. The heart-shaped track is pointed and around 2 inches wide. If the trail passes through woods with trees bearing nuts, look for squirrel ramblings. Their front footprint shows four toes with sharp claws. The rear print has five toes. If the squirrel was running or jumping, the rear prints are ahead of the front ones.

A game, especially exciting for young children, may be made by trying to identify what animals have been on the trail. The game involves identifying the supposed intruder by the track it leaves. The track is circumstantial evidence, since the actual animal has not been seen. This detective-type game may be made as simple or as difficult as desired. Take an animal track guidebook with you.

Lake Houston Wilderness Park: Peach Creek Loop and Forest Trail

Nature, creek, and forest lovers will find Lake Houston Wilderness Park untamed and ready for exploration. The nearly 5,000 acres contain heavy forests, creeks, and a lake that furnish prime habitat for birds, mammals, snakes, insects, and plants. Follow this trail through woods and along Peach Creek to experience a wild and natural environment within 30 miles of Houston.

Start: Park office on park road
Distance: 2-mile lollipop
Approximate hiking time: 1.5 hours
Difficulty: Easy due to flat trails and good shade
Trail surface: Dirt
Seasons: Year-round
Other trail users: Dog walkers
Canine compatibility: Leashed dogs permitted
Fees and permits: Small entrance fee per person age 13–65
Schedule: Gate open 8 a.m.–8 p.m. Sun–Thurs, 8 a.m.–10 p.m. Fri–Sat. Office hours 8 a.m.–5 p.m. every day.

Maps: Trail maps available at the park office; USGS: Moonshine Hill, Splendora
Trail contacts: Park Manager, 22031 Baptist Encampment Rd., New Caney 77357; (281) 354-6881; Houston Parks and Recreation Department (HPARD), 2999 South Wayside Dr., Houston 77023; (713) 865-4500; www.houstontx.gov/parks/trails.html
Other: Restrooms and water available near the trestle bridge. This is the only City of Houston park that offers camping facilities. The park is a game preserve.

Finding the trailhead: From downtown Houston take I-45 North to the exit for Beltway 8 East. Merge onto Beltway 8 East and proceed 5.8 miles east, then merge onto US 59 North, toward Cleveland. Follow US 59 North for 16 miles and then take the TX 1485/New Caney exit. After 0.5 mile turn right onto FM 1485 East. After 1.9 miles turn right onto Baptist Encampment Road and follow the Lake Houston Park signs for 1.6 miles to the park entrance at 22031 Baptist Encampment Rd. Follow the park road for about 1 mile to the paved parking area near the park headquarters. *DeLorme: Texas Atlas & Gazetteer:* Page 72, G1. GPS: N30 8.327' / W95 10.330'

THE HIKE

Note: Major new trail construction was planned for 2010. Check with park rangers for current trail information.

Reach the Peach Creek Loop Trail trailhead by following the park road east from the park office and over the metal and wood trestle bridge. This bridge, with Peach Creek and its sandy beach 15 feet below it, presents a photo op. It is the only trestle bridge in the park system, so bragging rights are in order for crossing it. Use insect repellant to ward off mosquitoes and other pesky insects. Watch for the many bird species, especially in the lowland areas, which have been identified as site 34 on the Texas Parks & Wildlife Upper Texas Coastal Birding Trail. Many hikers will remember when this was a state park from 1992 until 2006, at which time it became a Houston City Park. It is one of the most underutilized parks in the Houston area.

Start the Peach Creek Loop Trail at the trailhead just right of the end of the bridge, where the ends of the loop connect. Take the right branch, heading south with the woods on the left and Peach Creek on the right. Peach Creek flows south through the park until it meets Caney Creek to form good flat-water canoeing. Cross a wooden bridge over a shallow gully that channels water to the creek. At

The trestle bridge over Peach Creek, in Lake Houston Wilderness Park, is the only trestle bridge in the park system.

Lake Houston Wilderness Park: Peach Creek Loop and Forest Trail

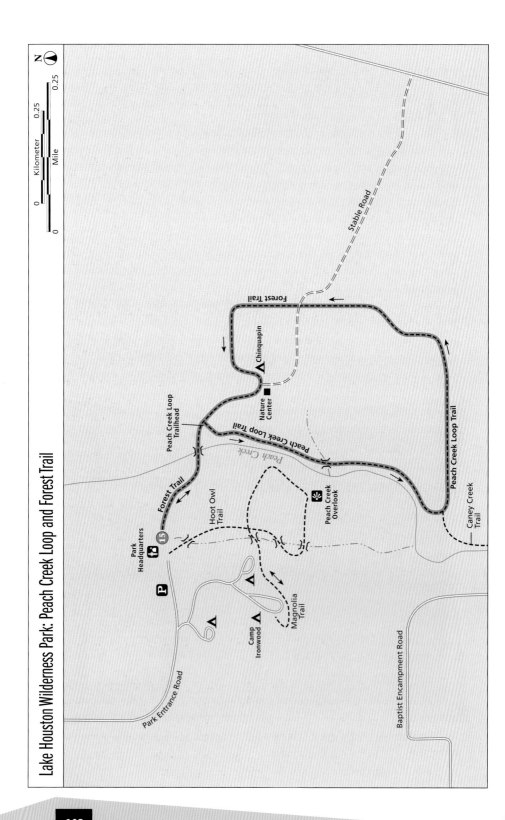

this point the creek is shallow and 80 feet wide. A wooden bench is on the right, with several paths down to the sandy shore. Use caution when straying off the trail, since water moccasins and copperheads, both venomous snakes, call this home. Prior to hiking, study a snake guidebook to enable you to recognize these snakes so that everything that slithers doesn't evoke fear and screams.

Continue following the trail as it initially parallels the creek and then heads away. Reach a 25-foot-long wooden bridge over a gully. The creek alternates from being easily seen to being hidden by the woods. When near the edge of the creek, look for river birch trees. They are easy to recognize by their papery, peeling bark. The trail has a few slopes up and down as it meanders through the woods. Follow the trail until reaching a Y, then take the left branch, *still heading south*. Pass a bench on the right that furnishes shade and a good view of the creek. The trail is now 25 feet above the creek.

In less than 0.25 mile, reach another Y. Take the left branch to remain on the Peach Creek Loop. The trail bends hard left, heading east and away from the creek. The woods are thick, and birds may be heard any time of the year. Listen for the tapping of woodpeckers, as five species nest here. In the fall notice the colorful display created by the red hand-shaped leaves of the sweet gum tree. Continue following the trail east until reaching a Y. Take the left branch, making a hard left and heading north. Pass a sign on the right pointing to the equestrian trails, and within a short distance pass a sign pointing to the hike and bike trails. Follow the trail, bearing left through the woods until reaching a bridge.

Cross the bridge, heading west into a clearing and onto the Forest Trail, which is an asphalt road. This is the Chinquapin area, which includes a campground and a nature center. It's worth a small detour to investigate the nature center, which includes live snake displays. George Mitchell, founder and developer of the Woodlands community north of Houston, funded the construction of the center. Return to the Forest Trail and head north until reaching the trestle bridge. Take a little time to relax and explore the sandy beach area below the bridge.

Backtrack from the trestle bridge to end the hike at the park office.

MILES AND DIRECTIONS

0.0   Start at the park office and take the park road south and then east to the Peach Creek trestle bridge.

0.2   Cross the trestle bridge and reach the Peach Creek Loop Trail trailhead, which is to the right at the end of the bridge. Take the right branch, heading south (GPS: N30 8.251' / W95 10.205'). In a couple hundred yards, cross a wooden bridge over a shallow gully. There is a bench on the right. Peach Creek is also on the right, about 5 feet away. Pass three steps on the left that lead to an open area with benches and a shelter.

0.4 Reach a 25-foot-long wooden bridge labeled #2. Bear right at the end of the bridge, still going generally south. There are steps on the right leading down to a beach alongside the creek. Follow the trail until reaching a Y and take the left branch, heading away from but still paralleling the creek.

0.5 Bear left at a trail marker post, still heading generally south.

0.7 Pass a marker post labeled PEACH CREEK TRAIL. In a short distance reach a Y and take the left branch, remaining on the Peach Creek Loop, HEADING EAST. The right branch leads to the Caney Creek Trail and a primitive campground.

0.9 Reach a Y and take the left branch, heading generally north. Pass a wooden bench and bear slightly right.

1.0 Reach another Y and take the left branch, still heading north.

1.2 Come to a Y and take the left branch, still heading north because the trail has wandered right and left.

1.3 Cross over Stable Road, a park maintenance road, and continue north, passing an equestrian trail on the right (east).

1.4 Pass the hike and bike trail on the right (east). Follow the Peach Creek Loop into the woods and bear left, still heading north.

1.7 Reach a wooden bridge at the end of the woods that curves to the right over a gully. At the end of the bridge is a mowed area where the Forest Trail, Chinquapin Camp, restrooms, a shelter, and a nature center are located. The Forest Trail is an asphalt road.

1.8 Veer off the Forest Trail to the left (south) and explore the nature center. Return to the Forest Trail and turn left, heading west. Continue following the Forest Trail as it bends to the right (north), until it reaches the trestle bridge.

2.0 Backtrack and end the hike at the park office.

Just a Brush Pile

I was just finishing raking up leaves and branches from the previous night's windstorm when Bob, a ranger friend of mine, greeted me. He asked if we were still on to hike this afternoon. I answered, "Let me finish breaking down this brush pile." He looked puzzled and asked why I wanted to break down the pile. I replied, "So it will fit in trash bags, so the trash crew will take it." His answer was quick and seemed logical: "Don't tell me that you, the great out-doorsman, are not leaving that brush pile in your yard?" I answered that I was getting rid of it because it cluttered the yard.

Bob volunteered to help me build a brush pile. He suggested we build the pile at the end of the yard near the corner of the fence. I said that would be fine, and it would also be out of view of the neighbors. As he was picking up some branches, he informed me, "You'll be amazed at how many birds, small mammals, and insects a good brush pile attracts. In some cases it's more interesting than a bird feeder." He then told me that the storm did some of the work, but we'd need some 4- to 6-foot-long and about 6-inch-diameter logs. Fortunately, I had a few I was saving to cut up for firewood.

He showed me how to lay the bottom layer of logs to form a base about 15 feet in diameter, with each log about 6 inches apart. We worked together

placing the second layer at right angles to the bottom layer, again with space between the logs. This was continued until the stack was about 3 feet high, when I called for a rest break. "What happens from here?" I asked. Bob replied, "When we finish the pile, it should be mound or tepee shaped. As we work toward the top, smaller branches may be used, and maybe we'll make a roof with some evergreen or discarded Christmas tree branches."

I thought a moment and commented that the pile still may be unsightly. Bob assured me the pile need not be obtrusive and suggested a "pretty up the pile" technique that included planting morning glories, clematis, or other blooming vines around the edges. He encouraged me by saying, "These vines will soon climb over the pile and turn it into a hill of flowers. The flowers will attract more birds and insects, including butterflies." The pile was beginning to sound extremely interesting to me. "Is there anything I should do or be looking for as the pile matures?" I asked.

Bob said to look around and into the edges of the pile for insects, spiders, toads, and salamanders and to keep a journal so I could record changes. He also noted that a brush pile furnishes resting and escape zones from predators for rabbits, small birds, and other critters. He finished by saying, "It's really a sight to watch when a hawk visits your yard and to see the small birds diving for the brush pile." I nodded my head and said, "We've done enough for today. Thanks for the help and education, and what about the hike?" Bob smiled and replied, "Why don't we hike Kleb Woods? They have some excellent brush piles."

Sheldon Lake State Park: Pond Loop, Bent Pine, and Swamp Rabbit Trails

This may be the nearest trail to Houston to see alligators—only 19 miles from downtown. The 49-acre Environmental Learning Center area is the heart of the hiking trails, even though the park contains 2,700 acres. Interconnecting trails, decks, and bridges over and around 27 former fish-rearing ponds furnish diverse habitats and excellent bird-watching. The ponds have naturalized and now support shorebirds, giant bullfrogs, water plants, and alligators. This is a great, easy hike for families with young children.

Start: Pond Loop Trail trailhead near the learning center

Distance: 1.5 miles of interconnecting loops with an out and back

Approximate hiking time: 1.5 hours to allow observation time

Difficulty: Easy due to flat trails

Trail surface: Decomposed granite

Seasons: Year-round

Other trail users: Bird-watchers, dog walkers, school groups

Canine compatibility: Leashed dogs permitted. Keep pets away from pond edges, due to alligators.

Fees and permits: None required

Schedule: Learning center open daily 8 a.m.–5 p.m.; closed Christmas Day and New Year's Day

Maps: Trail maps available at the park office; USGS: Jacinto City

Trail contact: Manager, Sheldon Lake State Park & Environmental Learning Center, 15315 Beaumont Hwy., Houston 77049; (281) 456-2800; www.tpwd.state.tx.us

Other: Learn alligator etiquette. Do not go into the ponds, and stay back from the water's edge. Free catch-and-release "family fishing" is permitted Sat–Sun only, for children accompanied by adults, in the two fishing ponds.

Finding the trailhead: Heading northbound on Beltway 8, proceed under the overpass of US 90 (Crosby Freeway) for 0.25 mile and take the JCT90 (Business) exit. Turn right on Business 90 (Beaumont Highway) and head east for 2 miles to Park Road 138. Look for the flagpole on the north side of the road. There is also a brown highway sign on the right. Turn left over the railroad tracks to the park entrance. Park headquarters is located at the learning center at 15315 Beaumont Hwy. *DeLorme: Texas Atlas & Gazetteer:* Page 131, C12. GPS: N29 51.492' / W95 9.663'

THE HIKE

S top at the park office to pick up a trail map. This large color-coded map is one of the best. Along with other information, the map has estimated hiking times for each trail. This park is a model for alternative energy use and conservation practices. Take time to see some of the exhibits/demonstrations. The Pond Loop Trail is 9 feet wide, surfaced with decomposed granite. It is wheelchair and stroller accessible. Use insect repellant to discourage the mosquitoes and other pesky insects, and apply sunscreen because the tree canopy and shade are intermittent. Benches are placed conveniently around the ponds.

Start the hike at the Pond Loop Trail trailhead across Park Road 138 near the Pond Center learning center. There is a large map board at the trailhead. This structured hike weaves around the ponds, each with its own distinctive character. They have been allowed to naturalize for more than 20 years and present an amazing amount of individuality. The ponds are not spring-fed, but rely on rain and runoff water, so their depth is dependent on the amount of recent rainfall.

Take the left (south) leg at Heron Plaza, heading southwest. The south-side ponds, the only ones visible from this section of trail, are designated by an S after their number on the map and their ID markers at the trail's edge. Immediately pass Ponds 1S and 2S, which are youth fishing ponds that can be used on weekends for catch and release. A trail comes in from the left at the west edge of Pond 2S. Take this short out-and-back path to get a closer view of Ponds 2S and 3S and Aquatic Lab 2. This floating deck over the water is used as an outdoor classroom and is an excellent place to safely observe pond life, including water striders and water boatmen.

The grass is mowed from the path's edge for about 5 feet down to the pond. Do not go in the water and stay back from the water's edge. Keep leashed pets

Sheldon Reservoir

Sheldon Reservoir was constructed in 1942 by the federal government to furnish water for industries along the Houston Ship Channel, which were providing goods for World War II. The reservoir is located on Carpenter's Bayou, which is a tributary of Buffalo Bayou about 19 miles east of downtown Houston. The Texas Parks & Wildlife Department acquired the reservoir in 1952 and designated it as the Sheldon Wildlife Management Area. It was opened in 1955 and became a state park in 1984. One of its first uses was as a fish hatchery. It is now Sheldon Lake State Park, and the fish-rearing ponds have been allowed to return to a more natural state.

away from the water, too—alligators reside in some of these ponds. If alligators are partially submerged, they may be difficult to see and they can lunge several feet. They are not a serious threat—just use common sense and alligator etiquette to enjoy them. Alligators semi-hibernate during the winter. They are most active in the spring and when bearing their young. Good photo ops may be available. Return to the Pond Loop Trail and turn left.

The numerous varieties of water lilies that grow in the ponds furnish resting spots for frogs and dragonflies. Watch for red, blue, and green varieties of dragonflies, especially during the summer. They will be hovering like helicopters and then speedily pick a mosquito out of midair. Cattails and water lilies are among the most prevalent plants. Pond 4S has become filled with young trees and presents new species of aquatic life. At the west edge of Pond 5S, turn left onto a path that forms a U, using a bridge to cross the pond and then return to the Pond Loop. Take a little time to read the information signs at the observation area in the middle of the bridge. Once back on the trail, pass a bridge that connects the north and south legs of the Pond Loop Trail. Pond 10S has the floating deck. Water shields, small oval plants with green leaves, cover much of the pond. Ducks and geese eat the seeds, leaves, and stems.

Sheldon Lake State Park is one of the few places near Houston where the roseate spoonbill can be seen. This magnificent bird, with a 4-foot wingspan, is exciting to watch.

Sheldon Lake State Park: Pond Loop, Bent Pine, and Swamp Rabbit Trails

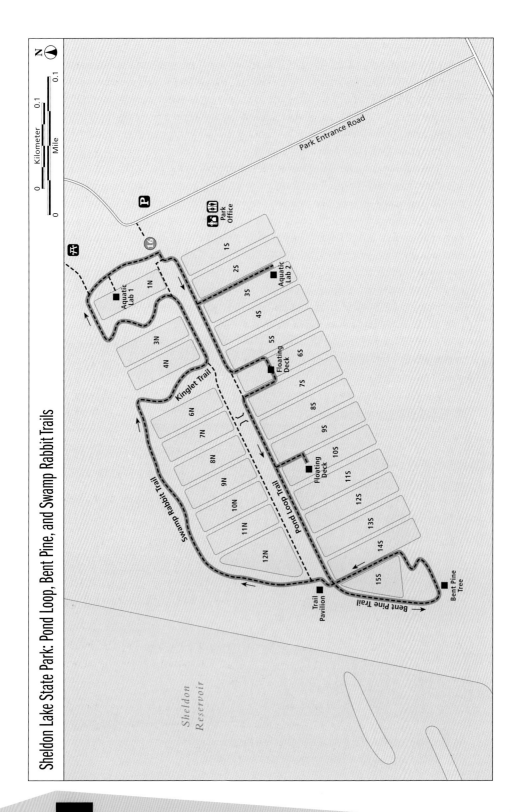

At the Y at the end of the south-side ponds, take the left branch, which is the Bent Pine Trail that forms a counterclockwise loop. Look for the bent pine, which was malformed by a large tree falling on it during a storm. Pass between Ponds 14S and 15S. Watch for roseate spoonbills, a large (up to a 4-foot wingspan), wide-billed bird with patches of rose-colored feathers. This is only one of the 250 species of birds found in the park. The Bent Pine Trail ends at a T, and there is a pavilion straight ahead. The pavilion is made from recycled material.

At the pavilion proceed to the Swamp Rabbit Trail, along the north-side ponds. Try to identify the many hardwood trees, including oak, cypress, and sycamore. Reach a long boardwalk going across a swampy area that can have mosquitoes. Follow a gradually rolling path until reaching a Y, and turn right onto the Kinglet Trail. There are several information signs along these trails. This short connector quickly reaches a T with the north side of the Pond Loop Trail. Take the left branch, heading toward Heron Plaza. Almost immediately turn left onto the Armadillo Trail. This short connector heads north to reach a T with the Swamp Rabbit Trail. Turn right and go past Aquatic Lab 1. Bear right and follow the trail back to the trailhead.

MILES AND DIRECTIONS

0.0 Start from the south Pond Loop Trail trailhead at the Pond Center and head southwest.

0.1 Follow the Pond Loop for 400 feet and turn left (south) on an out-and-back path that leads to Aquatic Lab 2, located in Pond 3S.

0.2 Return to the Pond Loop and turn left, heading west. Pass Ponds 4S and 5S on the left. Turn left (south) onto the path after Pond 5S and follow it as it passes between Ponds 5S and 6S.

0.3 Follow the path as it turns sharply to the right, heading west and leading across a bridge. At the end of the bridge, turn hard right, heading north. Reach the Pond Loop and turn left (west).

0.4 Pass Ponds 7S, 8S, and 9S and then turn left off the Pond Loop onto the out-and-back path leading to the floating deck.

0.5 Return to the Pond Loop and turn left, heading west and passing Ponds 10S through 13S.

0.6 Reach a Y adjacent to Pond 14S and take the left branch, heading west onto the Bent Pine Trail (loop). The right branch continues the Pond Loop. Almost immediately reach another Y where the ends of the Bent Pine Trail loop join. Take the right branch, bearing south. Pond 15S is on the left.

0.7 Follow the trail, making a hard left turn and heading east. Go past the sign identifying the bent pine tree. Follow the trail as it turns left and right and then make a hard left, heading north. Pond 15S is on the left, and Pond 14S is on the right.

0.8 Reach a T, which ends the Bent Pine Trail loop. Head straight ahead toward the pavilion and immediately reach a Y. Continue straight to start the Swamp Rabbit Trail. The hike may be shortened by taking the right branch, which is the northern leg of the Pond Loop Trail.

1.0 Continue following the Swamp Rabbit Trail, heading north and then bending right (east). Use the wooden boardwalk to cross a wet area and reach a Y. Take the right branch onto the Kinglet Trail, a point-to-point connector, heading south.

1.1 At the T take the left branch, heading east on Pond Loop Trail. Pass Ponds 4N and 3N on the left and then turn left onto Armadillo Trail, heading north. Armadillo Trail is a point-to-point connector trail.

1.2 Reach a T (this ends the Armadillo Trail) and take the right branch onto the Swamp Rabbit Trail, heading east. Follow the Swamp Rabbit Trail a short distance to where it ends at a Y with the Outdoor Access Route. Take the right branch, heading south past Aquatic Lab 1, the restrooms, and back to the trailhead.

1.5 End the hike at the Pond Loop Trail trailhead.

Armand Bayou Nature Center: Karankawa Trail and Prairie Platform

Follow the trails and the center's 600-foot-long interpretive boardwalk through three ecosystems. At Armand Bayou Overlook, watch out over the water for shorebirds, including egrets, cormorants, and ospreys. While winding through the woods, listen for the sounds of the more than 220 bird species that live here. At the Prairie Platform, gaze over one of the last remaining prairies in the Houston area. This is an outstanding hike for families with young children due to the live exhibits and discovery areas.

Start: Boardwalk behind park entrance building

Distance: 2.3 mile lollipop with an out and back

Approximate hiking time: 1.5 hours

Difficulty: Moderate due some rough sections of trail

Trail surface: Boardwalks, crushed limestone, dirt

Seasons: Year-round

Other trail users: School groups involved in nature study

Canine compatibility: Dogs not permitted

Fees and permits: Small entrance fee (age 3 and under free)

Schedule: Tues–Sat, 9 a.m.–5 p.m.; Sun, noon–5 p.m. Last admission at 4 p.m.

Maps: Trail maps available at the park office; USGS: League City

Trail contact: Armand Bayou Nature Center, 8500 Bay Area Blvd., Pasadena 77507; (281) 474-2551; www.abnc.org

Other: Restrooms and water fountains are located at the interpretive building. No bicycles allowed beyond the entrance building, where there is a bicycle rack available. Jogging is not allowed.

Finding the trailhead: From southeast Houston at the intersection of I-45 and Beltway 8, take I-45 South and travel 6 miles. Take the Bay Area Boulevard exit, turn left, and proceed 6 miles to the Armand Bayou Nature Center entrance at 8500 Bay Area Blvd. Park in the parking area and walk through the park gate to the entrance building. Lock your vehicle. *DeLorme: Texas Atlas & Gazetteer:* Page 72, K2. GPS: N29 51.492' / W95 9.663'

Stop at the entrance building to pick up a map and field checklist of birds. The hike starts from the rear of the entrance building. The Karankawa Trail trailhead is 0.2 mile southwest. Use insect repellant to discourage the mosquitoes and other pesky insects, and apply sunscreen because the tree canopy and shade are intermittent. Benches are placed conveniently along the trail. Allow time to see some of the live animal exhibits and read the educational signage, which ranks with the best. The live animal exhibits include snakes, spiders, and hawks.

Follow the 600-foot-long boardwalk as it goes into the woods, over swampy ground, across a pond, and ends at the interpretive building. At the pond there is a shelter and numerous educational signs. Linger in this area, and in all but the winter months, watch for turtles sunning themselves, dragonflies skimming the water for mosquitoes, bullfrogs announcing their presence, and small fish looking for food. Alligators also like the pond, so use proper alligator etiquette. Sometimes the gators are difficult to see as they lie semi-submerged in the water, with just a portion of their head and eyes visible. A trail sign and large map are located outside the interpretive building.

At the T at the Karankawa trailhead, take the right branch, heading southwest to walk the loop counterclockwise. The trail is wide, hard-packed soil and relatively flat. Once off the boardwalk, stay on the marked trails. Wandering from the trail can cause damaging erosion, trampling of native plants, and confusion for other hikers. Venomous snakes, such as copperheads and water moccasins, and nonvenomous snakes, such as garter snakes and black-banded water snakes, call this home. Prior to hiking, study a snake guidebook so you don't panic at everything that slithers. The ability to recognize various snakes can also add another dimension to the hike. This front portion of the trail is also called Boat House Road because it leads to the boathouse on Armand Bayou.

At about 1 mile into the hike, take the short out-and-back path that leads to the Bayou Overlook for a great view of the bayou and good photo ops. Sandbars and logs provide resting spots for various waterbirds, including ospreys, egrets, and cormorants. Watch for laughing gulls, a bird the size of a crow, with a black head, white neck, and gray back. They nest in colonies along marshes. Alligators also enjoy the bayou. Look for animal tracks along the bayou's sandy shore—white-tailed deer and armadillo will be the most numerous. Return to the Karankawa Trail and head south. Three wooden bridges will be crossed during the hike.

Watch for Spanish moss trailing from some of the trees. The woods include black gum, elm, ironwood, and white oak. There are also some loblolly pines. In the fall, American beautyberry shrubs furnish violet-colored berries to birds and mammals. The Central Flyway, the largest migratory bird route in North America, passes over these forested wetlands. Over 370 bird species have been spotted here. It is also a transition zone between mixed hardwoods, coastal prairie, and coastal salt marsh, providing excellent wildlife habitat.

After completing the Karankawa Trail loop and reaching the interpretive center, take the trail to the Prairie Platform. The platform is about 8 feet high and 175 feet long. One side faces remnant prairies. Returning from the platform to the interpretive center, pass by the Martyn Farm, containing several farm buildings representative of those of the 1800s.

Until the nineteenth century, this area was the hunting grounds of the Karankawa, Attakapa, and Cohuilletan Indian tribes. Large piles of oyster shells, called shelf middens, are the main archaeological remains of these peoples.

Armand Bayou was named in honor of Armand Yramategui, a Basque (an independent province in Spain) immigrant who used his self-made fortune to promote conservation in the Houston area. He pioneered the purchase of what would become the Armand Bayou Nature Center.

The Prairie Platform, on the Prairie Trail, furnishes an excellent view of a natural prairie, much like those of a century ago.

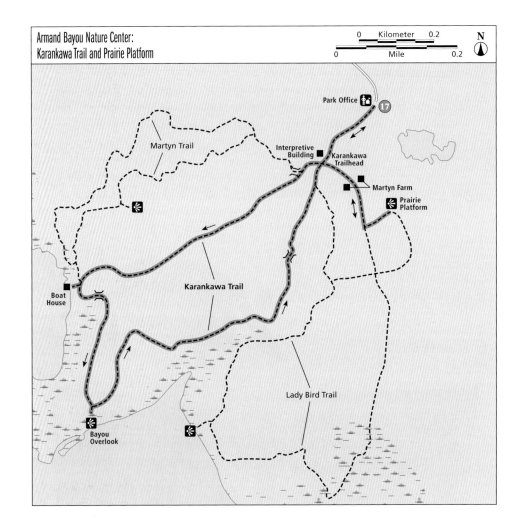

0   Kilometer   0.2

0   Mile   0.2

N

Park Office   17

Martyn Trail

Interpretive
Building   Karankawa
Trailhead

Martyn Farm

Prairie
Platform

Boat
House

Karankawa Trail

Lady Bird Trail

Bayou
Overlook

MILES AND DIRECTIONS

0.0   Start at the "teaching boardwalk" behind the entrance building.

0.2   Follow the boardwalk as it bears right and left over the swamp and pond until reaching the interpretive building (nature center). At the rear of the interpretive building, reach the Karankawa Trail trailhead. Head southwest and then bear left into the woods.

0.2   Pass by a trail that intersects from the right. This is the Martyn Trail. Continue following the Karankawa Trail southwest.

0.5   Pass a wooden bench on the left and some downed trees in the woods.

0.7 Continue on the trail past a small graveled area on the left containing a picnic table. Pass a trail marker on the right, where the Martyn Trail intersects the Karankawa Trail. Continue straight (the Karankawa Trail bears left) down a slope to the boathouse and bayou. Return to the Karankawa Trail and bear right, heading south.

0.8 Bear left and cross a wooden bridge over a gully (creek). Bear right and pass a bench on the right.

1.0 Reach a path on the right (west) that leads down to the Armand Bayou. Follow it to the edge of the bayou, where there are wood benches and an overlook. Return to the Karakawa Trail and follow it to the right, heading south.

1.3 Pass a trail marker post and at the bench on the right, bear left.

1.6 Follow the trail as it curves north, then east, and then north again. Cross a wooden bridge spanning a shallow gully.

1.7 Reach a T and take the right branch, heading north toward the nature center. This is the trailhead for the Karankawa Trail.

1.8 Reach the nature center. This finishes the Karankawa Trail. Go past the John P. McGovern Children's Discovery Area toward the gravel road.

1.9 Follow through the mowed grass and past the Martyn Farm buildings on the left. Take the Prairie Interpretive Trail and Short Loop Trail, heading south. Reach a path intersecting from the left (east) and take this path to the Prairie Platform.

2.0 Follow the raised Prairie Platform to the observation deck at its midpoint, then continue following the platform to its end. Take the trail past the platform to backtrack to the Martyn Farm. Pass by a water tank and windmill on the right. Continue toward the nature center.

2.1 Reach the interpretive building and backtrack on the boardwalk to the entrance building.

2.3 End the hike behind the entrance building.

> 🐾 **Green Tip:**
> *Carry a reusable water container that can be filled at any water tap. This saves money, since bottled water is expensive. Plus, lots of petroleum is used to make plastic bottles, and they're a disposal nightmare.*

Jesse Jones Park: Judy Overby Bell Trail

It's always great to find a new trail, but this one is unique. Opened in June 2009, it is one of the trailheads for the Spring Creek Greenway project that, via a series of trails along Cypress Creek, will ultimately connect Jesse Jones Park in Spring to Burroughs Park in Tomball—a distance of 32 miles. A bonanza for hikers! The tree-lined trail features an overlook at the junction of Spring Creek and Cypress Creek. Wildlife, including shorebirds near the creek, is abundant.

Start: Trailhead adjoining pavilion parking lot on west side of park

Distance: 2.2 miles out and back

Approximate hiking time: 1.5 hours

Difficulty: Easy due to flat terrain and modest tree canopy

Trail surface: Crushed aggregate

Seasons: Best Sept–June

Other trail users: Cyclists, wheelchairs, strollers

Canine compatibility: Dogs not permitted

Fees and permits: None required

Schedule: Jan and Dec, 8 a.m.–5 p.m.; Feb and Nov, 8 a.m.–6 p.m.; Mar–Oct, 8 a.m.–7 p.m. Park and nature center closed Thanksgiving Day, Christmas Eve, Christmas Day, and New Year's Day.

Maps: Trail maps available at the park office; USGS: Maedan

Trail contact: Park Manager, Jesse Jones Park, 20634 Kenswick Dr., Humble 77338; (281) 446-8588; www.hcp4.net/jones

Other: Park entrance closes and gates are locked 30 minutes prior to posted hours. No swimming in ponds or creeks. No potable water available on the trail.

Finding the trailhead: From north Houston at the intersection of I-45 North and North Sam Houston Parkway East, merge onto North Sam Houston Parkway East. Travel 5.5 miles and merge onto Sam Houston Parkway East. Continue 4.7 miles and then merge onto US 59 North, toward Cleveland. In 0.3 mile take the exit toward FM 1960 (west). Go 0.1 mile and turn left onto FM 1960BR/W. Follow FM 1960 for 3.2 miles and turn right onto Kenswick Drive. Follow Kenswick to the park entrance at 20634 Kenswick Dr. Pick up a map at the nature center then park in the playground parking lot. *DeLorme: Texas Atlas & Gazetteer:* Page 71, H12. GPS: N30 1.567' / W95 17.909'

THE HIKE

O ne of the exciting things about this hike is that it is one of the first connector trails that will join Jones Park with Burroughs Park in Tomball, creating 32 miles of hiking. Watch for the numerous plant identification markers that can enhance your outdoor experience. Since few hikers have discovered the Judy Overby Bell Trail, there is a degree of seclusion not available in some city hikes. The trail is wheelchair and stroller accessible. It is a multiuse trail, but the 10-foot width allows room for everyone. Use insect repellant to discourage the mosquitoes.

The trail heads northwest and then bends west to where it currently ends. Cypress Creek, often not visible, parallels the right (east and north) side. Enter into the woods with trees and undergrowth on both sides. At times the tree canopy

> *Poison ivy is a member of the cashew family. Many species of birds and other wildlife enjoy eating the small red berries during the summer and fall. All sections of the plant cause uncomfortable allergic reactions in most humans.*

Mushrooms and toadstools can be seen in spring and fall along the Judy Overby Bell Trail. Many mushrooms are poisonous—do not even touch them.

Jesse Jones Park: Judy Overby Bell Trail

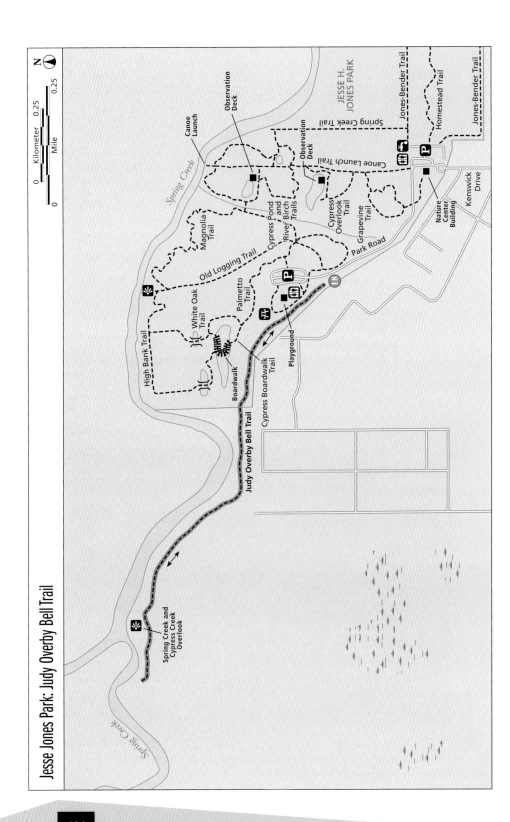

N

Kilometer
0   0.25

Mile
0   0.25

Spring Creek

Canoe Launch

Observation Deck

JESSE H. JONES PARK

Jones-Bender Trail

Spring Creek Trail

Homestead Trail

Jones-Bender Trail

Observation Deck

Canoe Launch Trail

Cypress Overlook Trail

Grapevine Trail

Magnolia Trail

Cypress Pond and River Birch Trails

Old Logging Trail

Nature Center Building

Kenswick Drive

Park Road

White Oak Trail

Palmetto Trail

High Bank Trail

Boardwalk

Playground

Cypress Boardwalk Trail

Judy Overby Bell Trail

Spring Creek and Cypress Creek Overlook

Spring Creek

is dense, furnishing welcome shade during the summer. Pass by American holly shrubs, easily identified by their identification markers and their glossy green leaves, small whitish flowers in the spring, and bright red berries in the fall (the berries are poisonous). Holly is widely used in Christmas decorations. There is a plant identification marker near the holly. Parts of a subdivision privacy fence and house rooftops may be seen to the left, through the trees.

The woods, numerous drainage channels to Cypress Creek, and the creek itself furnish ideal habitat for many species of birds and other wildlife. Listen for the spring chorus of the small but loud male tree frogs, hoping to draw the attention of a female. They are especially active in early evening. The raucous call of the blue jay—a piercing *jay, jay, jay*—may be heard as this large bully dives to frighten other birds from feeding areas. Continue following the trail, generally northwest, as it wanders a bit to the right and left.

Reach a small clearing, identified as a pocket prairie. Various wildflowers, including black-eyed Susans, may be seen in the spring. Painted lady butterflies, having reddish orange wings with black tips, may be seen drinking at mud holes near the trail in the spring and early fall. These medium-size butterflies are often mistaken for the slightly larger monarch butterfly. There are several visual distractions around the clearing, including overhead power lines, a small substation, a subdivision, and a park maintenance road. Follow the trail, bearing left from the clearing.

The trees surrounding the trail change to predominantly oaks, including red, post, and white. Go by a large white oak tree identified by a sign. Cross over a metal culvert carrying the water from a 10-foot-wide drainage channel to the creek. Reach a Y and take the right branch, which has a deep gully to its right. A large residence can be seen to the left. Bear left at a plant identification sign for sweet gum and almost immediately pass a sign identifying southern magnolia. The park boundary fence is about 150 feet away to the left.

Reach the overlook where Spring Creek and Cypress Creek join. This is the high point of the hike and provides good photo ops. It is possible to go to the edge of the cleared area, where the creeks are 15 feet below.

Stay in the cleared area or on the trail because water snakes, including the nonvenomous black-banded and venomous water moccasins, live by the creek and the woods. In the spring and fall, look along the creek shores for great blue herons and snowy egrets. These are both large birds and often stand in shallow water looking to have a fish dinner. The trail currently ends a short distance from the overlook. Backtrack to the trailhead.

0.0 Start from the trailhead adjoining the pavilion parking area and head right (northwest).

0.1 Pass plant identification signs: American holly on the right and American beautyberry and greenbrier on the left.

0.2 Reach a clearing and see a subdivision to the left, power lines overhead, and a power substation on the right. Continue following the trail going left, then right as the trail bears northwest.

0.3 Pass an overgrown jeep road and a chain-link fence on the left, about 50 feet away.

0.4 Cypress Creek is to the right but cannot be seen. Several drainage channels on the right lead to the creek, about 35 feet away.

0.5 Follow the trail over a large metal culvert that helps channel water from a 10-foot-wide drainage canal to the creek. Pass a plant identification sign for sassafras and then reach a Y and take the right branch, heading northwest.

0.9 Continue following the trail as it zigzags. Pass a plant identification sign for sweet gum and in a short distance pass an identification sign for southern magnolia. The park boundary fence is about 150 feet away, to the left.

1.0 Reach a cleared area that leads to the creek overlook. Cypress Creek and Spring Creek are on the right and join at this point. A path leads to the overlook, which is about 15 feet above the creeks.

1.1 A locked gate and a fence end the trail. Backtrack to the trailhead.

2.2 End the hike at the trailhead.

This hike is great for nature lovers and families with young children. Follow a boardwalk and then cross over a cypress swamp featuring an observation deck. Continue over another small pond and through a red bay grove to the Spring Creek Overlook. See the largest bald cypress tree in Harris County. Enjoy a small bamboo grove amid large hardwoods, while watching for birds and wildlife.

Start: Palmetto Trail trailhead, adjacent to northwest side of playground parking area

Distance: 1.8 miles out and back with a small loop

Approximate hiking time: 1.25 hours

Difficulty: Easy due to flat terrain and modest tree canopy

Trail surface: Asphalt

Seasons: Best Sept–June

Other trail users: Bird-watchers, wheelchairs, strollers; cyclists and mountain bikers on Sun only

Canine compatibility: Dogs not permitted

Fees and permits: None required

Schedule: Jan and Dec, 8 a.m.–5 p.m.; Feb and Nov, 8 a.m.–6 p.m.; Mar–Oct, 8 a.m.–7 p.m. Park and nature center closed Thanksgiving Day, Christmas Eve, Christmas Day, and New Year's Day.

Maps: Trail maps available at the nature center; USGS: Maedan

Trail contact: Park Manager, Jesse Jones Park, 20634 Kenswick Dr., Humble 77338; (281) 446-8588; www.hcp4.net/jones

Other: Restrooms and a water fountain are located in a separate building north of the nature center. No potable water available along the trails. Park entrance gate closes 30 minutes before posted closing. No swimming in ponds or creeks. No skateboards allowed on the trails.

Finding the trailhead: From north Houston at the intersection of I-45 North and North Sam Houston Parkway East, merge onto North Sam Houston Parkway East. Travel 5.5 miles and merge onto Sam Houston Parkway East. Continue 4.7 miles and merge onto US 59 North, toward Cleveland. In 0.3 mile take the exit westward toward FM 1960. Go 0.1 mile and turn left onto FM 1960BR/W. Follow FM 1960 for 3.2 miles and turn right onto Kenswick Drive. Follow Kenswick to the park entrance at 20634 Kenswick Dr. Pick up a map at the nature center then park in the playground parking lot. *DeLorme: Texas Atlas & Gazetteer:* Page 71, H12. GPS: N30 1.669' / W95 17.875'

S ign in and pick up a trail map at the nature center. There is a large trail map mounted near the nature center entrance. Restrooms and drinking water fountains are available in a separate building adjacent to the nature center. Drive to the playground parking area and park on the northwest side. Use insect repellant and sunscreen, and wear a hat. The trail is wheelchair and stroller accessible, and the junctions and intersections along the route are well marked. Benches are placed appropriately along the trail. The Palmetto Trail trailhead is adjacent to the parking area, on the northwest side.

Follow the Palmetto Trail as it bends right and left through the mixed hardwoods and loblolly pines. Watch for information signs identifying various trees and plants. A few dwarf palmetto trees, sometimes just a single tree and then a small group, can be seen. Encounter several Y junctions that are well signed, and generally follow left, while heading north or northwest. Look for American beautyberry bushes, which can be 5 feet tall and grow singly or in groups. Their leaves have white wooly undersides, and between June and August small clusters of bluish flowers are present. In the fall small, bright purple fruits furnish food for birds.

The Palmetto Trail leads to the Cypress Boardwalk Trail. Look for the sign identifying Alabama supplejack and then watch for these vines as they climb small trees. The vines bear small, greenish white flowers from April through June and blue fruits from July to October. There are some near the redbud tree information sign. After 0.5 mile reach the boardwalk over the cypress swamp. The boardwalk is about 6 feet above the swamp. It is 6 feet wide but has no rails, so keep young children in tow.

After the boardwalk, follow the trail to the left, heading north, and then make a hard right and cross over a bridge. Watch for a very large bald cypress tree. This Harris County champion has a diameter greater than 4 feet. It will be necessary to tilt your head back to see to the 110-foot top. The most common tree in this area is the water oak. The mature trees can be 50 feet tall, with a 2- to 3-inch diameter. The leaves are wedge shaped and broadest near the tip. Continue following the trail north, until reaching a small path intersecting from the left, leading to the Spring Creek Overlook.

The short out-and-back hike to the overlook furnishes good photo ops. Great blue herons and white egrets may be seen standing patiently in the shallow water, waiting to catch an unsuspecting fish or frog. Stay on the marked trails to avoid encountering poison ivy or snakes. The park furnishes a home to more than twenty species of snakes, including the venomous water moccasin. Sometimes snakes may be seen along the water's edge or sunning in tree limbs above the water. Learn to identify the venomous snakes so that seeing a nonvenomous snake can add an extra dimension to the hike—without the fright.

Head east on the High Bank Trail, with the creek on the left. Wind through the woods, passing a small patch of bamboo, surrounded by large magnolia trees. Reach a T with an old logging trail and backtrack to the White Oak Trail. The north branch of the logging trail leads to Spring Creek. At the White Oak Trail turn left, heading south. Cross a bridge over a swampy area and follow left at the Y and then south, until intersecting with the Cypress Boardwalk Trail. Backtrack to the trailhead to end the hike.

The observation deck over the cypress swamp furnishes great photo ops, including the magnolia tree arching over the deck.

Jesse Jones Park: Palmetto, Cypress, High Bank, and White Oak Trails

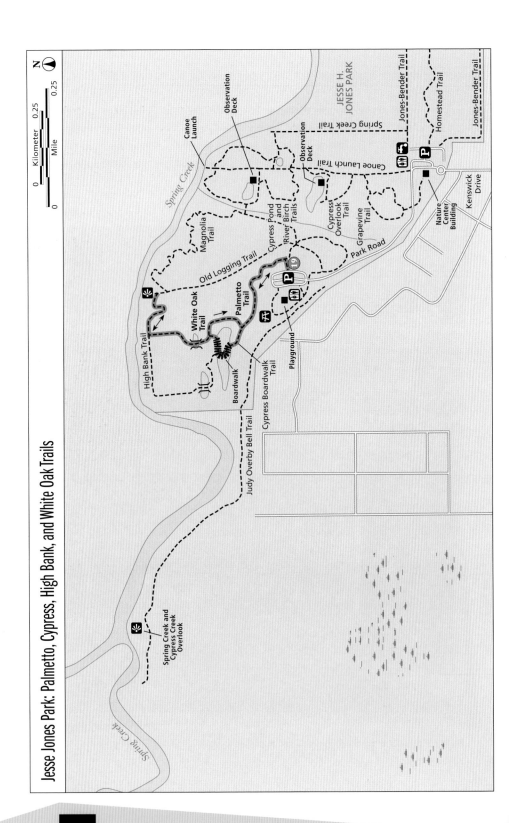

0.0 Start from the Palmetto Trail trailhead adjacent to the playground parking area on the northwest side. Turn left and head north.

0.1 At a Y junction, take the right branch, continuing on the Palmetto Trail heading north. In less than 100 yards, come to a Y and take the left branch, heading northwest.

0.3 Reach a T and take the left branch onto the Cypress Boardwalk Trail. The curving boardwalk over the pond has an observation deck. Turn right (east) at the end of the boardwalk for a scant 100 yards.

0.4 Continue on the Cypress Boardwalk Trail and bear left, away from the pond. Join the White Oak Trail, which comes in from the right.

0.5 Continue north on the White Oak Trail and reach a wooden bridge over a small pond.

0.7 Bear right, then left, and reach a T with the High Bank Trail. Turn right, heading east.

0.9 Follow the High Bank Trail until it reaches the old logging trail and the Spring Creek Overlook. Turn around and backtrack to the bridge over the small pond.

1.3 At the Y intersection with the White Oak Trail, take the left (east) branch as it loops around the larger pond and intersects with the Palmetto Trail. Continue backtracking.

1.8 End the hike at the trailhead.

Jesse Jones—Visionary

The Jesse H. Jones Park & Nature Center was made possible by the Houston Endowment Foundation's donation of the first $25,000 for the park's development. The foundation was established by Jesse Jones and his wife, Mary Gibbs Jones, in 1937. Naming the park after Jones was not surprising, since neither Jones nor the foundation was modest about attaching his name to things that he funded.

Jesse Holman Jones (1875–1956) brought his family from Tennessee to Texas in 1892, hoping for a better life. It would have been hard for Jones to have imagined just how much better it would be. Jones was ambitious and eager for success. He wandered from job to job until he started to work for his uncle, who owned a lumber company. He soon became a manager there, and from that time on used his financial savvy, organizational talents, and determination to make Houston a top-ranking city. His efforts resulted in the construction of thirty-five of the city's first skyscrapers.

Jones's personal fortunes continued to grow from his involvement in the construction and building industries. He was the co-founder of Humble Oil Company, which later became Exxon. The profits from Humble Oil catapulted him into a position where he could make a major difference in Houston's development and stature. He helped develop the Houston *Chronicle* into a major newspaper and was also influential in building the San Jacinto Monument, which memorializes Sam Houston's defeat of General Santa Ana and the Mexican Army in the Texas Revolution.

One of Jones's lesser known, but major, accomplishments was his influence in completing the Houston Ship Channel. The channel was started in 1902 and not completed until 1914. This 50-mile waterway connects Houston to the Gulf of Mexico. Today, thanks to the channel, Houston is a major port.

On the national scene, Jones served two presidents. President Woodrow Wilson appointed him director general of the American Red Cross during World War I. President Franklin D. Roosevelt selected him as head of the very powerful Reconstruction Finance Corporation in the 1930s during the Great Depression.

Jesse H. Jones is probably the one person most responsible for giving Houston the foundation to make it the city it is today.

Jesse Jones Park: Canoe, Cypress Overlook, River Birch, and Spring Creek Trails

This hike is for lovers of ponds, swamps, woods, creeks, and wildlife. It combines several trails, while exploring some of the best features of the park. Pass by a small pond where several species of turtles may be fed. Cross another pond to reach Spring Creek and see a clay bluff that is the highest point on the creek. Continue near the creek, watching for snakes, including venomous water moccasins, along the banks.

Start: Canoe Launch Trail trailhead, across park road from nature center

Distance: 1.9 miles of interconnecting loops

Approximate hiking time: 2.25 hours

Difficulty: Moderate due to some elevation changes and sandy sections of trail

Trail surface: Asphalt, sand, dirt

Seasons: Best Sept–June

Other trail users: Bird-watchers; wheelchairs and strollers for a portion of the trail; cyclists and mountain bikers on Sun only

Canine compatibility: Dogs not permitted

Fees and permits: None required

Schedule: Jan and Dec, 8 a.m.–5 p.m.; Feb and Nov, 8 a.m.–6 p.m.; Mar–Oct, 8 a.m.–7 p.m. Park and nature center closed Thanksgiving Day, Christmas Eve, Christmas Day, and New Year's Day.

Maps: Trail maps available at the nature center; USGS: Maedan.

Trail contact: Park Manager, Jesse Jones Park, 20634 Kenswick Dr., Humble 77338; (281) 446-8588; www.hcp4.net/jones

Other: Restrooms and a water fountain are located in a separate building north of the nature center. No potable water available along the trails. Park entrance gate closes 30 minutes before posted closing. No swimming in ponds or creeks. No skateboards allowed on the trails.

Finding the trailhead: From north Houston at the intersection of I-45 North and North Sam Houston Parkway East, merge onto North Sam Houston Parkway East. Travel 5.5 miles and merge onto Sam Houston Parkway East. Continue 4.7 miles and merge onto US 59 North, toward Cleveland. In 0.3 mile take the exit toward FM 1960. Go 0.1 mile and turn left onto FM 1960BR/W. Follow FM 1960 for 3.2 miles and turn right onto Kenswick Drive. Follow Kenswick to the park entrance at 20634 Kenswick Dr. Park in the parking area opposite the nature center. *DeLorme: Texas Atlas & Gazetteer:* Page 71, H12. GPS: N30 1.427' / W95 17.666'

S ign in and pick up a trail map at the nature center. Packaged turtle food may be obtained for a small monetary donation. There is a large trail map mounted near the nature center entrance. Restrooms and drinking water fountains are available in a separate building adjacent to the nature center. Use insect repellant and sunscreen, and wear a hat. The Canoe Launch Trail trailhead is across the park road. Junctions and intersections along the route are well marked. Most of the trail is wheelchair and stroller accessible.

In less than the length of a football field, reach a Y. Take the left branch, heading west onto the Grapevine Trail. This short counterclockwise loop trail leads through heavy woods that include red mulberry, basswood, and sweetleaf hardwood trees and loblolly pines. Watch for the muscadine grape vines that climb up some trees. The blue grapes ripen in late summer and make excellent jelly, but are too tart to eat raw. Look overhead to possibly glimpse a red-shouldered hawk. They make gentle circles, sometimes gliding on the wind, in their search for food, which includes mice, birds, frogs, and snakes. These hawks are easily recognized by their reddish head, shoulders, and belly, with dark brown wings. Their cry of *kee-ah, kee-ah* is loud and distinct. Complete the loop at the Y that joins the ends of the trail and take the connector path back to the Canoe Launch Trail.

A great white egret seems suspended in midair as it prepares to land in tree tops near Spring Creek.

In a short distance reach a Y and turn left, heading northwest onto the Cypress Overlook Trail. The trees furnish good shade and at times form an arch above the trail. Pass a path on the left that leads to a wildlife-viewing blind. Prior to reaching the turtle-feeding deck, pass a very large, 4- to 5-foot diameter and 70-foot-tall magnolia tree. At the end of the small pond is a deck that allows hikers to feed the turtles. Three species are in the pond: the red-eared slider, Mississippi mud turtle, and common snapping turtle. They are eager eaters and can be viewed every season except winter. The Cypress Overlook Trail dead-ends into the Canoe Launch Trail.

Head north on the Canoe Launch Trail until reaching a crossover where the Cypress Pond and River Birch Trails cross Canoe Launch. There is a trail marker indicating that Spring Creek is straight ahead (north), the River Birch Trail heads west and east, and the Cypress Pond Trail heads east. Turn left, taking the River Birch Trail west. The woods reach to each side of the trail. The understory is not dense, affording an opportunity to "see" into the woods. Follow the trail as it weaves through the trees.

There is a short out and back to the Cypress Pond observation deck. Depending on the amount of recent rainfall, the pond may be a swamp. This is a great place to kick back and enjoy, while resting on the benches on the deck. The deck is 15 feet above the swamp and has a huge magnolia tree bending over it. It's a good spot for photos. Follow the trail east, back to the Canoe Launch Trail, and then turn left, heading north. The concrete canoe-launching area is a good place to get to the shore of Spring Creek. Look for great blue herons and white egrets fishing along the creek. These birds are about 2 feet tall, with slender long beaks and legs.

After leaving the launch area, head southeast, taking the trail along the creek. This is not an "official" park trail, but gives good views of the creek and connects to the River Birch Trail, which leads back to the Canoe Launch Trail. Follow the Canoe Launch Trail for 0.3 mile south, back to the trailhead.

The Springs of Santa Rosa

Across from Jesse Jones Park, just upstream from where Spring Creek runs into the San Jacinto River, lies a freshwater spring on a high bluff that naturalists and anthropologists believe to be the Springs of Santa Rosa as discussed in historical accounts of Spanish explorers. The Springs of Santa Rosa was once home to the Akokisa Indians who lived in the region. Although anthropologists have not yet explored it, the spot is a registered historic site with the Texas Historical Commission. Unfortunately, the land was recently sold to a developer, and the future of the spring is uncertain.

Jesse Jones Park: Canoe, Cypress Overlook, River Birch, and Spring Creek Trails

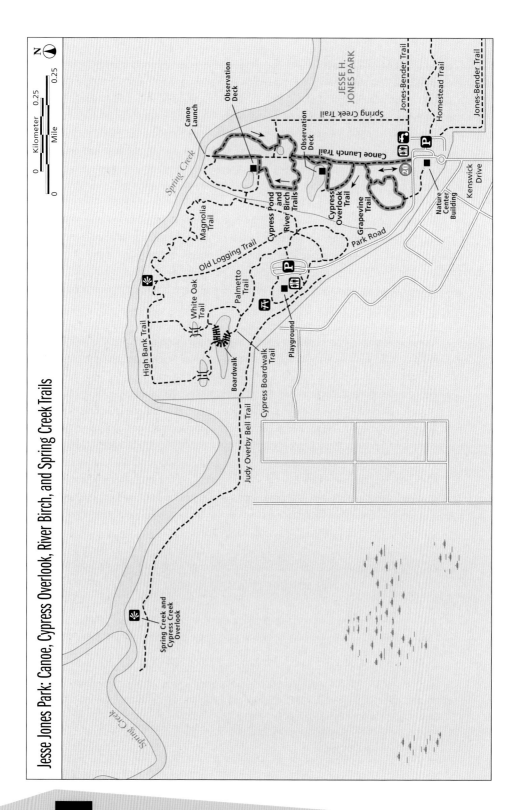

0.0 Start from the Canoe Launch Trail trailhead adjoining the parking area in front of the nature center and head right (north). Follow the Canoe Launch Trail for less than 0.1 mile and reach a Y. Take the left branch, heading west onto the Grapevine Trail. The right branch is the Canoe Launch Trail.

0.1 Reach a Y and take the right branch, bearing west to go counterclockwise around the loop.

0.2 Keep bearing left, following the Grapevine Trail. You'll pass a short connector back to the nature center. Continue to the left around the loop.

0.3 Follow the trail east and then make a hard left, heading north. In less than 0.1 mile reach the Y where the loop started. Take the right branch, which is a short connector back to the Canoe Launch Trail.

0.4 Turn left (north) back onto the Canoe Launch Trail. Almost immediately come to another Y. Turn left, heading west on the Cypress Overlook Trail. Bear right in a large semicircle.

0.7 Reach a path coming from the left. Take the path over a bridge to a pond overlook with benches and information signs about turtles. Go back to the Cypress Overlook Trail on the opposite (north) side of the observation deck.

0.8 Reach the T with the Canoe Launch Trail. Take the left branch, heading north, and immediately reach a Y. Take the left branch, heading west onto the Cypress Pond and River Birch Trails.

1.0 Follow the trail, which forms a semicircle to the right. Reach a short out-and-back path to an observation platform at the edge of the cypress swamp (sometimes a pond).

1.1 Return to the Cypress Pond Trail and proceed left (east) until reaching the T with the Canoe Launch Trail. Take the left branch, heading north.

1.2 Reach the canoe-launching area, which is concrete. This section along Spring Creek is not wheelchair or stroller accessible.

1.3 Come back up the concrete area and turn left (east) onto a sandy unnamed trail following Spring Creek. The creek is on the left (north). Continue following the trail along the creek.

1.4 Reach a Y and take the right branch, heading generally south into the woods.

1.5 Follow the trail and undulate up and down until reaching a T at the top of an uphill slope. Take the left branch. There are trail markers pointing to the River Birch Trail and the nature center.

1.6 Continue following the River Birch Trail until reaching a Y. There is no signage here, but take the right branch, which bears southwest. Within 0.1 mile reach a T with the Canoe Launch Trail. Take the left branch and backtrack south to the trailhead.

1.9 End the hike back at the trailhead.

The shell or skin of a cicada is shed after the insect leaves its burrow to become an adult.

21

Primitive Trail. The hike can be extended by nearly 2 miles by taking the Primitive Trail Loop. Head back toward the Lily Pond. After reaching the pond, backtrack to the trailhead by the visitor center. Although the trails have marker posts, it is easy to repeat parts of the many loops. If this happens, just enjoy the woods and its creatures, using the Lily Pond as a reckoning point.

Thelma and Charles Mercer's dream of sharing their small personal garden with the community was achieved in 1974, when the Harris County Precinct 4 Parks Department preserved the property. The arboretum has now grown to 300 acres.

> *The bald cypress tree is known by many names, but "casket tree" is probably the weirdest. Its resistance to decay and therefore its use in caskets prompted this name.*

The fountain in the Lily Pond is a welcome sight, especially during the heat of summer.

Mercer Arboretum: East Oxbow and Little and Big Cypress Loops

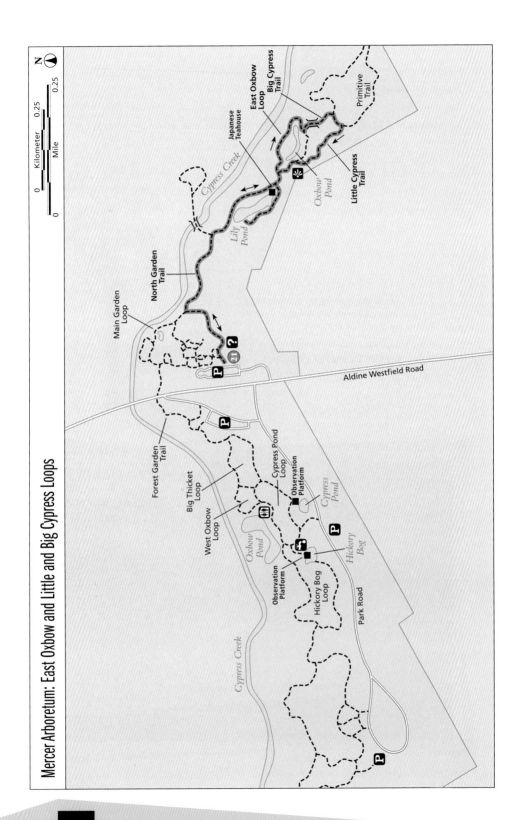

North

0 — Kilometer — 0.25

0 — Mile — 0.25

Main Garden Loop

North Garden Trail

Japanese Teahouse

Cypress Creek

East Oxbow Loop

Big Cypress Trail

Primitive Trail

Little Cypress Trail

Lily Pond

Oxbow Pond

Forest Garden Trail

Big Thicket Loop

West Oxbow Loop

Oxbow Pond

Cypress Creek

Aldine Westfield Road

Cypress Pond Loop

Observation Platform

Cypress Pond

Observation Platform

Hickory Bog Loop

Hickory Bog

Park Road

the Texas Master Naturalist–Heartwood Chapter for partici-
pating in the Mercer Adapta Trail program and maintaining
sections of the trail. Continue on the trail through the woods
until reaching a Y, where a water fountain is located. Follow
the left branch, heading south on the Hickory Bog Loop Trail.
Curve left until reaching the wooden observation deck. The bog
may have standing water or be dry, depending on the amount
of recent rainfall. The end of the deck facing the water has no
guardrail, making observation of the various insects, frogs, and possibly
a water snake easier. Some of the plants in the bog are labeled—look for the Loui-
siana iris. There are many trees in the swamp, including hickories and water elms.
Scanning the area with a set of binoculars can add to the visual aspect of the hike.

Leave the observation deck and follow the Hickory Bog Loop until joining
the Cypress Pond Loop. The trail meanders from right to left, sometimes making a
small semicircle, as it heads generally east.

Bear left and take the left branch of the Y, which is the West Oxbow Loop.
Watch for a bench on the left that overlooks the oxbow that was created by the
wanderings of Cypress Creek. This is a great spot to observe wildlife, including butterflies, frogs, birds, and large turtles. Return to the trail and within 0.1 mile reach
a restroom on the left. This is about halfway through the hike. Take the left branch
of the next Y, which parallels the oxbow gully. Watch for red bay trees and yaupon
holly. The leaves of the red bay are the common spice called bay leaves.

At the next intersection, follow the left branch east onto the Big Thicket Loop.
Pass some mowed grass clearings and watch for large trees, including loblolly
pines more than 3 feet in diameter and 90 feet high. Cross a short bridge and make
a hard left at the end of the bridge. In a short distance reach a Y and take the right
branch, heading south to the Jake Roberts Maple Trail. The main parking area is on
the left, and there is a small shelter next to the trail with water fountains for both
humans and dogs. Notice the young trident maples planted as a memorial. This
area is mowed, and benches are conveniently placed. Continue following the trail
over a bridge. At the T take the left branch, which is the Cypress Pond Loop, and follow it to a Y. Immediately reach the Cypress Pond boardwalk and observation deck.
Spend some time here simply enjoying the pond. Leave the observation deck and
follow the edge of the pond, heading west and then south to the trailhead.

MILES AND DIRECTIONS

0.0 Start from the Bald Cypress Swamp trailhead across the park road from the
Cypress Swamp/Hickory Bog parking area on the west side of the park.

0.1 Reach a Y and take the left branch. Follow the trail, curving left to the
observation platform by the Hickory Bog.

Mercer Arboretum: Cypress Pond, Hickory Bog, Oxbow, and Big Thicket Loops

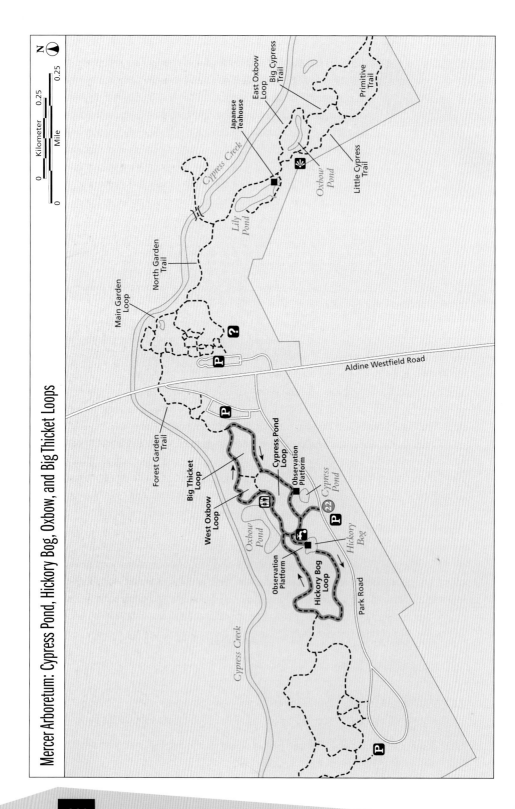

N

0 Kilometer 0.25

0 Mile 0.25

Cypress Creek

North Garden Trail

Main Garden Loop

Lily Pond

Japanese Teahouse

East Oxbow Loop

Big Cypress Trail

Primitive Trail

Oxbow Pond

Little Cypress Trail

Aldine Westfield Road

Forest Garden Trail

Big Thicket Loop

West Oxbow Loop

Cypress Pond Loop

Observation Platform

Cypress Pond

Oxbow Pond

Hickory Bog

Observation Platform

Hickory Bog Loop

Park Road

Cypress Creek

22

0.2 At the end of the boardwalk, bear left and go up a slight grade. Pass a path on the left that leads to the park road. Continue following the trail generally to the west.

0.4 Reach a Y and take the right branch. Bear right and left while following the trail.

0.7 Pass a path on the right that leads to the Hickory Bog boardwalk. Continue straight and then left to reach a bench overlooking the creek. Return from the bench and upon reaching the trail turn left, heading northeast.

0.8 A wooden structure housing a restroom is on the left. Just beyond the restroom reach a Y and take the left branch, heading toward the Cypress Creek oxbow. A narrow path to the left leads to an overlook of the oxbow.

0.9 Pass by a large mound of earth, about 10 feet high, on the left. Bear right at the end of the mound, then hard left and back right.

1.0 Reach a T and take the left branch. The right branch leads back to the Cypress Pond Loop, the West Oxbow Loop, and the restrooms. Pass a path on the left that leads to a bench about 20 feet away. Continue following the trail eastward and cross a wooden bridge over a gully. Take a hard left at the end of the bridge, then continue straight ahead.

1.1 Reach a Y and take the right branch toward the Jake Roberts Maple Collection. Curve to the right and pass a small shelter containing a water fountain. There is a path on the left leading to the main parking lot. Make a sharp right and continue following the trail through the Jake Roberts Maple Collection.

1.2 At the end of the Jake Roberts Maple Collection, reach a short wooden bridge over a gully. Continue straight until reaching a T, then take the left branch toward the Cypress Pond Loop.

1.4 Bear right and reach a Y and the entrance to the Cypress Swamp observation deck. Take the left branch, following around the swamp to the Bald Cypress Swamp Trailhead.

1.5 End the hike at the Bald Cypress Swamp trailhead.

What's an Oxbow?

I was with a couple of my granddaughters, Nikki (age 14) and Jessa (age 12), taking a leisurely hike on the west side of Mercer Arboretum. We had passed the Hickory Bog, then we reached a small path leading to a park bench overlooking a shallow gully. The sign by the bench identified the gully area as an oxbow left by Cypress Creek. It was obvious the creek had moved farther north, isolating the oxbow. The word *oxbow* piqued the girls interest. "What's an oxbow?" they asked.

I told them oxbows are lakes, usually crescent shaped, alongside slow-moving rivers or creeks, like the Cypress. They looked down into the gully and said, "We don't see much of a lake." I replied, "That's because we've been in a drought, and oxbows can temporarily dry out without rain or floodwater."

I then told them that a lazy river can change its course when the original channel hits rock, hard soil, or any other impediment. This causes the river to start to form a loop, and over time erosion and deposits of soil help the river cut a new channel. The water on the inside of the loop travels slower, forming deposits of silt. The outside edges tend to flow faster, eroding the banks and making the neck of the loop even wider. Eventually this meandering channel widens until the neck vanishes. This section of meandering stream is isolated from the river's channel, and through the work of nature, an ox-yoke-shaped oxbow lake is formed.

"How long does this take?" the girls asked. I answered, "No one knows. It depends on a lot of variables. It could happen fairly quickly or take years." Since the lake has no current, sediment gradually builds up along the banks and fills in the lake. We're lucky to be able to observe an oxbow lake, almost in our backyard. Another neat thing about oxbow lakes is that they can support fish and other aquatic life. Many times the fish that are living in the oxbow are not common in the river or creek's active channel. Also, wood ducks, beavers, deer, turtles, frogs, and other animals live near the lake.

I mentioned that many of our natural lakes here in the South are actually oxbows that lie in a favorable floodplain. They all came from a river or creek at some point. This information caught the girls' attention and Nikki asked, "Do you mean like Lake Jackson?" "Exactly," I replied, "Lake Jackson is an oxbow."

I then told them that oxbows are dynamic and, like most things, have a limited lifespan. Weather extremes, such as floods and drought, can slow or hasten this span, though that may take centuries. Nikki commented, "It sounds like an oxbow lake is constantly changing and eventually headed for extinction." I answered, "Extinction is pretty final. What happens is a natural process called progression. Over time the lake fills in and then it eventually turns into a wetland. Bushy undergrowth follows that, and finally a forest."

Amazed by Grandpa's knowledge, we headed back to the arboretum.

Collins Park: Gourley Nature Trail

It's always exciting to hike a new trail. But it's downright thrilling to hike on the first completed leg (dedicated in December 2008) of an eventual 32-mile trail along Cypress Creek. When finished, this series of connectors, trails, and parks will be part of the Cypress Creek Greenway project. This particular hike runs parallel to Cypress Creek with its abundance of wildlife, then circles a turtle-filled fishing pond in Meyer Park and backtracks to Collins Park.

Start: Trailhead on southeast side of parking area where Collins Park Trail joins Gourley Nature Trail

Distance: 1.2 mile lollipop

Approximate hiking time: 1 hour

Difficulty: Easy due to 10-foot-wide paved trail

Trail surface: Asphalt

Seasons: Year-round

Other trail users: Cyclists, strollers, wheelchairs, joggers, dog walkers, skateboarders

Canine compatibility: Leashed dogs permitted

Fees and permits: None required

Schedule: Mon–Fri, 7 a.m.–10 p.m.; Sat–Sun, 8 a.m.–10 p.m.

Maps: None available in the park; USGS Tomball

Trail contact: Harris County Precinct 4 Parks Department, 1001 Preston, Suite 924, Houston 77002; (281) 353-4196; www.hcp4 .net

Finding the trailhead: From the north side of Houston at the intersection of Beltway 8 and I-45 North, turn left onto Beltway 8 West. Continue on Beltway 8 West for 2.8 miles to Veterans Memorial Drive. Turn right onto Veterans Memorial Drive and proceed 4.1 miles to where Veterans Memorial Drive turns into Stuebner Airline Road. Follow Stuebner Airline for 1.9 miles until reaching Cypresswood Drive. Turn right onto Cypresswood and continue 0.4 mile to North Greenfield Drive. Turn right (south) onto North Greenfield Drive into Collins Park at 6727 Cypresswood Drive and park at the first parking area on the right. Lock your vehicle. *DeLorme: Texas Atlas & Gazetteer:* Page 71, H12. GPS: N30 0.593' / W95 30.623'

THE HIKE

The Gourley Trail trailhead is located southeast of the parking area and starts where the Collins Park Trail ends. Check out the trail map board on the right side. The trail is flat and 10 feet wide, with an asphalt surface suitable for wheelchairs and strollers. It is a multiuse trail, so keep right and be aware of cyclists approaching from the rear. Head south, going away from the parking area toward the woods. Cypress Creek is on the left (south) about 40 feet away, and the Collins Park skateboard area is on the right (north). Bear slightly right (southwest) and follow straight ahead around large trees that furnish intermittent canopy cover.

Go up a minor slope and cross a concrete bridge spanning a drainage ditch. Continue following the asphalt trail. This portion of the trail is made possible by an easement through private property. Do not stray off the trail. The left edge of the trail is flat for 10 feet and then drops sharply to Cypress Creek. Many of the hardwood trees have large vines growing on them. Watch for butterflies, dragonflies, and numerous species of birds. Spring and fall is the best time to see wildlife. The tree cover is intermittent, so wear a hat and take water. Hardwood trees are predominant, including water oak, with some scattered loblolly pines. Yaupon holly, an undesirable invasive, creates part of the understory.

Continue following the trail in a southwest direction until Stuebner Airline Road comes into view. There is a large billboard and utility lines on the right edge of the trail. Pass under the road, and leave Collins Park and enter Meyer Park. Immediately turn right (northwest), paralleling Stuebner Airline Road, and continue until making a hard left, heading west, away from the road. Reach a Y with a trail information board and map on the right. Take the right branch, still heading west. A large fishing pond is on the left. A few trees and mowed grass, including a picnic area, are on the right.

The pond is 15 feet from the trail, down a slight slope over short grass. This is a good point to detour down to the pond edge to observe some aquatic life, including water striders. Red-eared slider turtles may be seen sunning themselves on semi-submerged logs. They often slide off into the water upon sensing vibrations from footsteps. Return to the trail and turn left, heading west. Continue following

The caterpillar you find on a bush along the trail is probably a moth caterpillar. In Texas, moths outnumber butterflies 15 to 1.

the trail, bearing counterclockwise around the edge of the pond. There is good tree canopy here, furnishing welcome shade.

Make a sharp left turn, heading southeast, and reach a wooden bridge over a portion of the pond and an overflow stream. The entire pond and some of the Meyer Park picnic area and woods can be seen from the center of the bridge. Some catch-and-release anglers may be trying their luck against largemouth bass. There is a sign stating NO SWIMMING OR WADING ALLOWED. Cross over the bridge and go straight ahead until reaching a hard left turn (east/northeast). Woods are on the right, and the pond is on the left. Glimpses of Stuebner Airline Road may be observed through the trees. Squirrels, butterflies, and small birds may be seen and heard near the woods.

Reach a Y and take the left branch. The right branch is a Meyer Park trail. Continue heading northwest until closing the loop that led around the pond. Take the right branch and backtrack to the trailhead. After crossing under Stuebner Airline Road, the trail parallels Cypress Creek on the right. This area is teeming with wildlife, and the leisurely backtrack is a good time to make hiking notes.

The nature trail is named in honor of Genevieve and Robert Gourley, whose family donated a recreational easement through their property along Cypress Creek.

The Gourley Nature Trail leads to a fishing pond, where turtles may be seen sunning during all seasons, except winter. They dive into the water when they feel vibrations from folks walking.

Collins Park: Gourley Nature Trail

COLLINS PARK

Cypresswood Drive

North Greenfield Drive

Stuebner Airline Road

Cypress Creek

ELIZABETH KAISER MEYER PARK

🍂🌿 **Green Tip:**
Pack out your dog's waste or dispose of it in a trash can.
Small plastic bags are now being furnished at many trailheads.
Many trails now have ordinances that impose a fine
for leaving waste on the trail.

0.0 From the southeast side of the parking area where the Collins Park Trail joins the Gourley Nature Trail, head southwest on Gourley.

0.1 Continue following the trail in a westerly direction. Reach and cross a concrete bridge over a dry gully. Cypress Creek is on the left, about 10 feet away, after a sharp drop.

0.2 The Stuebner Airline bridge can be seen straight ahead. Continue toward the bridge.

0.3 Reach the bridge and follow the trail as it crosses under Stuebner Airline Road into Meyer Park. Cypress Creek is on the left (southwest). Make a right (northwest), then a hard left (west), and continue toward a Y.

0.4 Reach the Y and check out the trail board on the right. Take the right branch, heading west into the woods. This branch circles a large fishing pond on the left and is not part of the Gourley Nature Trail. The circle heads west, then south, then east, and then north to return to this spot.

0.5 Follow to the left along the edge of the pond until reaching a Y. Take the left branch, heading north toward the Gourley Nature Trail. The right branch is a Meyer Park trail.

0.6 Cross over a 50-foot-long wooden bridge that spans an overflow portion of the pond. Continue following the edge of the pond, with the pond on the left.

0.8 Reach the Y that joins the Gourley Nature Trail with the circular pond trail. Take the right branch onto the Gourley Nature Trail and backtrack to the trailhead.

1.2 End the hike back at the trailhead.

Collins Park: Cypress Creek Greenway

This trail is for creek lovers, and is one of the new Cypress Creek Greenway trails. It is an out-and-back trail, mostly along the creek, that presents two different views: one in the manicured playfield section of Collins Parks, and the other in the more natural biking trail along the creek. Cypress Creek overlooks provide good photo ops. Many species of birds may be seen, including groups of great blue herons and great white egrets.

Start: Cypress Creek Greenway Trail trailhead on the east side of east parking area

Distance: 1.8 miles out and back

Approximate hiking time: 1.25 hours

Difficulty: Moderate due to narrow trail and some minor elevation changes

Trail surface: Asphalt, dirt

Seasons: Year-round

Other trail users: Dog walkers, mountain bikers, joggers; wheelchairs and strollers on paved section

Canine compatibility: Leashed dogs permitted

Fees and permits: None required

Schedule: Dawn to dusk

Maps: None available in the park; USGS: Tomball

Trail contact: Harris County Precinct 4 Parks Department, 1001 Preston, Suite 924, Houston 77002; (281) 353-4196; www.hcp4 .net

Other: Mountain bikers use a portion of this trail. Keep to the right.

Finding the Trailhead: From the north side of Houston at the intersection of Beltway 8 and I-45 North, turn left onto Beltway 8 West. Continue on Beltway 8 West for 2.8 miles to Veterans Memorial Drive. Turn right onto Veterans Memorial Drive and proceed 4.1 miles to where Veterans Memorial turns into Stuebner Airline Road. Follow Stuebner Airline for 1.9 miles until reaching Cypresswood Drive. Turn right onto Cypresswood and continue 0.4 mile to North Greenfield Drive. Turn right (south) onto North Greenfield Drive into Collins Park at 6727 Cypresswood Dr. Park at the parking area on the east side of the park. Lock your vehicle. *DeLorme: Texas Atlas & Gazetteer:* Page 71, H12. GPS: N30 0.693' / W95 30.404'

THE HIKE

The Cypress Creek Greenway Trail trailhead is located on the east side of the east parking area. Check out the trail map board on the right side. The first 0.3 mile of the trail is flat, 10 feet wide with an asphalt surface, suitable for wheelchairs and strollers. It is a multiuse trail, so keep right and be aware of mountain bikers approaching from the rear. Head east, going away from the parking area, toward the fenced baseball fields. This section has no tree canopy, so use sunscreen, wear a hat, and take water (the water will be especially appreciated when backtracking). No potable water or restroom facilities are available along the trail.

A mother and son examine a pine cone to try to identify the species of pine tree it dropped from. Many of the linear trails have access from homes along the trail.

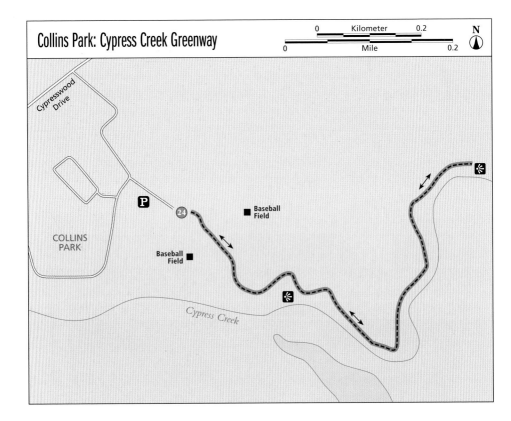

Follow the wide asphalt trail as it leads between two fenced baseball fields. Reach a Y and take the left branch into the woods and away from the ball field. The trail surface changes to dirt and narrows. The right branch continues around the ball fields. This section of the trail is most often used by mountain bikers. The woods are full of mature hardwood and pine trees. Reach another Y and take the left branch. The right branch leads down to Cypress Creek and is used by mountain bikers to ride along the creek. Follow the trail as it bears right and left and back again. It is very pleasant and quiet in the woods.

Reach the park boundary chain-link fence. Large residences may be seen past the fence and through the trees. Take the right branch, which stays close to the fence. Continue following the trail for about 0.1 mile, at which time no more homes can be seen, only woods on the other side of the fence. This area is a favorite of small birds, including warblers. Watch and listen for them as they flit back and forth among the trees. Try to identify the Carolina chickadee, which is present all year. This small (5-inch) bird is easy to identify with its black cap and chin and tan belly. It also identifies itself with its high-pitched, fast *chika-dee-dee-dee-dee* song.

Reach a Y and continue on the left branch, straight along the fence. The trail can have muddy spots after a rain. Glimpses of Cypress Creek can be seen on the right, through the woods. At about 0.5 mile into the hike, reach a Y and take the right branch. This is a short out and back to the Cypress Creek Overlook. A sandbar and some bubbling rapids can be observed from the overlook. Unfortunately, included in this view is a large drain culvert at the creek edge. This is a good resting spot, and some good photo ops are available. Return to the main trail and follow it along the creek as it lopes up and down.

A pair of elevated green pipes across the creek comes into view to the right. These pipes carry oil and natural gas. The creek comes into full view through a clearing. Great white egrets, large birds over 3 feet tall with a 4.5-foot wingspan, and great blue herons, which are somewhat larger, may be seen along the creek edge and flying about. These birds are more prevalent in the spring and fall. Reach a large clearing on the left, where two large residences, off the park property, can be seen. Cypress Creek is about 50 feet away to the right. Many narrow dirt bike paths crisscross the trail.

Continue straight ahead as the trail leads through a large group of native bamboo trees. These are easily recognized by their green bark with small ridges about every foot. Mature trees are about 1 to 2 inches in diameter and less than 15 feet tall. Reach a clearing on the right that furnishes a good view of the creek, which is down about 20 feet from the trail. There is a railroad tie placed along the right side of the trail. This is a good spot to rest, and some shade can be found to the left. Backtrack to the trailhead.

For the more energetic, the hike can be extended to T. C. Jester Road before backtracking. The Cypress Creek Greenway Trail system has added miles of trails for hikers to enjoy.

Green Tip:
Pack out what you pack in, including food scraps because they can attract wild animals and be detrimental to them.

0.0 Start from the Cypress Creek Greenway Trail trailhead adjacent to the east side of the east parking area in Collins Park. Head east on the asphalt trail.

0.25 Follow the asphalt trail bearing right, between fenced baseball fields. Reach a Y and take the left branch, which is dirt, heading into the woods and away from the ball fields. The right branch continues following along the baseball fields.

0.3 Reach a Y and take the left branch. The right branch is a short leg leading to Cypress Creek. Continue following this dirt bike trail until reaching the park boundary fence.

0.4 At the T at the fence, take the right branch and follow the fence line on your left. Cypress Creek is through the woods to the right but not visible. Reach a Y and continue straight, taking the left branch.

0.5 Reach a Y and take the right branch, which is a short out-and-back leg that leads to Cypress Creek Overlook. Creek rapids can be seen from this point. Return to the main trail and follow it as it veers left.

0.7 Go under two large green oil pipes that cross the creek. Pass a large clearing on the left. A few mansion-like residences can be seen to the left through the clearing, off the park property. Cypress Creek can be seen on the right. Pass through a large clump of bamboo.

0.8 Reach a Y and take the right branch, which follows the creek. A bike path crosses the trail.

0.9 Reach a clearing on the right that gives a good view of the creek. A railroad tie is next to the trail, and woods are on the left. This is a good spot to rest and then backtrack to the trailhead. The hike can be lengthened by following the trail to T. C. Jester Road and then backtracking.

1.8 End the hike at the trailhead.

Faulkey Gully Trail

This hike is representative of many of the new, linear, in-city trails in Houston. They are built along gullies, bayous, and floodplain property. One edge of the trail generally abuts a residential area shielded by fences, but with gates opening to the trail. This encourages hikers from the area to frequently use the trail. Several species of birds, including egrets, may be seen along the gully.

Start: Trailhead adjoining sidewalk and bridge on Lakewood Forest Drive

Distance: 1.6 miles out and back

Approximate hiking time: 1.25 hours

Difficulty: Easy due to paved flat surface

Trail surface: Asphalt

Seasons: Best Sept–July

Other trail users: Wheelchairs, strollers, cyclists, joggers, dog walkers

Canine compatibility: Leashed dogs permitted

Fees and permits: None required

Schedule: Dawn to dusk

Maps: No trail maps available; USGS: Satsuma

Trail contact: Harris County Precinct 4 Parks Department, 1001 Preston, Suite 924, Houston 77002; (281) 353-4196; www .hcp4.net

Finding the trailhead: From the northwest side of Houston at the intersection of US 290 West and West Sam Houston Parkway North, turn left (northwest) onto US 290 West. Travel 1.6 miles and turn right onto Jones Road. Follow Jones Road 5.3 miles to Grant Road. Turn left onto Grant Road and go 1.1 miles to Lakewood Forest Drive. For access to the trail, park in a small off-road parking area across from the Lakewood Residents Club at the intersection with Lake View Place. Lock your vehicle. *DeLorme: Texas Atlas & Gazetteer:* Page 71, I10. GPS: N29 59.408' / W95 35.593'

🌿 Green Tip:
Be mindful of and courteous to others. Many linear trails, along gullies and bayous, pass by residential areas. Avoid making loud noises and intruding on others' privacy.

THE HIKE

Start the hike heading northwest, with Faulkey Gully on the left. The trail is an 8-foot-wide asphalt multiuse trail. It is wheelchair and stroller accessible. Skaters, cyclists, and joggers also use it, so keep to the right and watch for bikes coming from the rear. There is no drinking water, tree cover, or shade—take water and a hat, and use sunscreen. The hike is best done on shady days.

Faulkey Gully is on the left, down a 20-foot slope and then another 5 feet down. It is 7 feet wide and generally shallow. A large—about 150 feet in diameter—retaining pond is on the right. This helps prevent flooding during periods of heavy rainfall as the water is funneled to the gully. Residences are on the right behind a wooden fence, 15 feet away. The right and left edges of the trail are mowed, with few trees or bushes. Tops of trees can be seen above the fence, in the homes' yards.

Watch and listen for birds flitting about the trees. Occasionally a barking dog may be heard from behind the fence.

White egrets may be seen near the gully or wading in its flowing water. It is interesting to watch these birds as they patiently wait, standing absolutely still, and then suddenly strike at a fish in the water. Even when the water is murky, they are amazingly accurate in catching small fish. In the spring and fall, turkey buzzards lazily circle in the sky, looking for carrion. These large black birds are not noted for their beauty.

On the right, utility lines follow and are behind the fence shielding the subdivision. Numerous culverts pass under the surface of the trail. These carry runoff water from many sources into the gully. Houses can be seen, sometimes through trees, on the left (southwest) of the trail.

Pass by a road from the subdivision that ends near the right side of the trail. There is a partial wooden barricade blocking the road. A sidewalk leads from the trail to the residences, affording another entry to the hike. This trail, like many of the linear trails created along bayous, streams, and other floodplain properties, encourages the people near it to use it. This offers many hiking opportunities to people who otherwise might have to travel to find a trail.

Faulkey Gully Trail is typical of linear trails (out and back), utilizing land along gullies that are designed for flood control.

Notice the long arching bridge over the gully on the left, leading to the Heatherwood Clubhouse. The clubhouse grounds are used by residents for swimming, tennis, and other athletic activities. On the right is a 75-foot-wide clearing with a sidewalk leading to the street. This area has some trees so offers a spot to leave the trail for a few moments to rest and get out of the sun. Also on the right edge of the trail is a wooden bench constructed by Boy Scouts from Troop 469. Continue following the trail—homes shielded by a privacy fences are on the right and the gully is on the left.

Continue straight ahead (north) and the Louetta Road bridge crossing the gully will be in sight. There is another bench on the right built by the Scouts. The gully is on the left, and this is its most accessible point. The left edge of the trail is flat for 5 feet and then gently slopes down 15 feet to the water's edge. Take a short out-and-back hike to explore what the stream offers. Use caution—after heavy rains the water can rise swiftly.

On the right side is a slanted concrete retaining wall. This is the end of this portion of the trail. Backtrack to the trailhead. For those wishing to extend the hike, a concrete path goes beneath the Louetta Road overpass.

MILES AND DIRECTIONS

0.0   Start from the trailhead adjoining the sidewalk and bridge on Lakewood Forest Drive. Head along the gully away from the trailhead.

0.3   Continue following the trail, bearing slightly to the left (northwest). Pass a sidewalk on the right that leads to a road in the subdivision and creates another entrance to the trail. A wooden barricade is at the end of the road.

0.6   Continue following the trail straight ahead (north) and pass a clearing on the right. The fence shielding the residences temporarily ends here and a sidewalk leads to the street, affording another entrance to the hike. On the left (west) a long arching bridge spans the gully and leads to the Heatherwood Clubhouse.

0.8   Continue north (straight ahead) on the trail until reaching Louetta Road. A concrete-paved underpass under Louetta Road allows safe passage. The hike can be extended for several miles by following the trail through the underpass. For this hike retrace your steps to the trailhead.

1.6   End the hike back at the trailhead.

Little Cypress Creek Preserve: Pond Loop Trail

This new hike is for pond lovers, wetlands aficionados, bird-watchers, and those folks with only time to hike on the weekends. The trail opened in 2009 and affords an easy, interesting, and refreshing hike. Several ponds allow easy access to investigate aquatic life. The wetlands habitat, including Little Cypress Creek, is perfect for the 140 species of birds, deer, and other mammals. The preserve is open on weekends.

Start: Pond Loop Trail trailhead at west edge of parking area
Distance: 1.3-mile loop
Approximate hiking time: 1 hour to allow time to explore the ponds
Difficulty: Easy due to relatively flat trail
Trail surface: Dirt and grass
Seasons: Best Sept–June
Other trail users: Dog walkers, bird-watchers
Canine compatibility: Leashed dogs permitted
Fees and permits: None required

Schedule: Sat and Sun, 9 a.m.–5 p.m.; closed Thanksgiving Day, Christmas Eve, Christmas Day, and New Year's Day
Maps: None available at the preserve; USGS: Cypress.
Trail contact: Harris County Precinct 4 Parks Department, 1001 Preston, Suite 924, Houston, TX 77002; (281) 353-4196; www.hcp4.net
Other: Sat is reserved for hikers, no cyclists; Sun for hikers and cyclists.

Finding the trailhead: From the northwest side of Houston at the intersection of West Sam Houston Parkway North and US 290 West, merge onto US 290 West. Follow US 290 West for 5.2 miles and then turn right onto Telge Road. Follow Telge Road for 3.4 miles and turn onto Spring Cypress Road. The park is at the intersection of Spring Cypress Road and Telge Road, fronting on Telge. Turn into the gravel parking area. Lock your vehicle. *DeLorme: Texas Atlas & Gazetteer:* Page 71, I11. GPS: N29 59.459' / W95 39.223'

The hike starts at the Pond Loop Trailhead at the west edge of the parking area. It is important to use insect repellant because in addition to mosquitoes, Rocky Mountain ticks thrive in this wetland. After completing the hike, check for any ticks clinging to your clothing. Apply sunscreen and wear a hat, since there is little tree canopy to provide shade. Several benches are placed conveniently along the trail. Traffic noise from Telge Road may be heard for the first 100 yards on the trail. The preserve is bordered by Telge Road, Little Cypress Creek, and a subdivision.

This trail is a favorite for bird-watchers, looking for some of the 140 species that have been recorded—an amazing number for a 60-acre area. A series of 10 shallow ponds were designed and created to mature into a functioning wetland. Three of the ponds are adjacent to the trail, allowing for easy observation of the pond life. Start the hike from the trailhead and immediately cross over a short bridge spanning a drainage ditch. Go through a cleared area, reach a Y, and take the right branch. There are two small ponds, one on each side of the trail. Take time to explore the pond on the right, which is used as an outdoor classroom and has several benches facing the water. The area around the ponds can be swampy.

At the Y, at the rear of the benches, take the right branch. Sections of the trail can be muddy after a rain. The trees, which up to now have been mostly hardwoods, including live oak and elm, change to mixed hardwoods and loblolly pines. Watch for birds flying near the ponds, including scissor-tailed flycatchers. The flycatcher, a medium-size bird, is easily identified by its extremely long black tail that has patches of white. Look for these birds in the summer as they sit in trees, waiting to pounce on some unsuspecting insect. Follow the trail as it undulates slightly up and down through the woods and swamp.

The woods change to mostly loblolly pines. There are many young trees that have been planted to help stabilize the soil and provide wildlife shelter. The trail surface becomes mostly grass and is about 7 feet wide. The hike generally follows a counterclockwise path. Reach a Y where residences can be seen straight ahead.

Green Tip:
Do not take souvenirs from along the trail home with you. This means natural material such as plants, rocks, bird feathers, and shells. If you find historic artifacts, including fossils and arrowheads, notify the park management or take them to the park office.

Take the left branch, heading northwest. Bear left, heading into the woods away from the houses. Look for cedar waxwings sitting in the trees. This sleek medium-size bird is gray to light brown and has a pointed crest that leads away from its distinct black mask. The birds enjoy juniper berries and are often seen in flocks.

Pass a narrow path that leads to Little Cypress Creek. Continue on the main loop trail as it bears left, then right, and then left again. Look for deer tracks in the sandy soil. Mostly small deer inhabit the area. In the fall look for acorns from the live oak trees. The acorns are small, dark brown, and often have lost their cap. Reach a Y and take the left branch, then immediately bear right. Continue forward and watch as the tree mix changes from oaks to pines. Go up and then down a slight elevation change.

Follow to the right as Little Cypress Creek comes into view. The creek has carved out a gully that slopes down about 8 feet. A bench along the creek provides a spot to rest. Little Cypress Creek effectively forms the west boundary of the preserve. This is a scenic portion, and birds are abundant. Bear left as a radio transmission tower comes into view. The last 0.1 mile is alongside noisy Telge Road, under high-power lines, but such are the visual and auditory distractions of some of the in-city hikes convenient to subdivisions.

A family group stops to investigate one of the many ponds along the Pond Loop Trail.

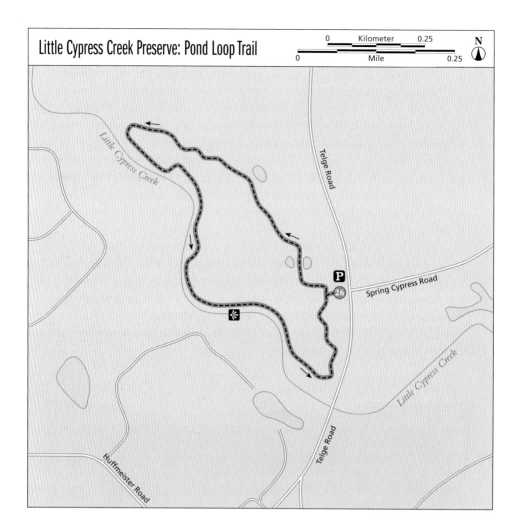

Little Cypress Creek Preserve: Pond Loop Trail

MILES AND DIRECTIONS

0.0 Start from the trailhead on the west side of the parking area. Head west, into the woods. Within 200 feet reach a Y. Take the right branch, bearing slightly north. Follow the trail to the right around a small pond on the left. Make a hard left and pass between the pond on the left and another pond on the right. Reach another Y and take the right branch, heading northwest.

Pioneers tapped the river birch tree in the spring to obtain its sweet sap, an ingredient in birch beer.

0.2 Pass a small pond on the right and reach a Y. Take the left branch, heading northwest. Residences will be in view. A short out-and-back path on the right leads to Little Cypress Creek. Return to the Pond Loop Trail and bear left.

0.4 Reach a Y and take the right branch. Continue following the loop as it bears generally left, west to south.

0.5 Reach a Y and take the left branch, heading south. The right branch dead-ends near a subdivision.

0.6 Reach a Y and take the right branch, heading southeast. Little Cypress Creek is on the right. Bear hard right and follow along the gully. The Little Cypress Creek Preserve chain-link boundary fence can be seen to the right, on the other side of the creek.

0.7 Pass a wooden park bench and reach a Y. Take the right branch, running along Little Cypress Creek. The woods are on the left.

0.9 Continue following the Pond Loop Trail and pass a radio transmission tower on the right. The tower is off the preserve property.

1.0 Reach a wooden bench that faces the creek. Bear right, heading south, with the creek on the right.

1.2 At a large pile of rocks bear left, heading north. The preserve boundary fence and Telge Road are visible straight ahead.

1.3 Continue following the trail north along the boundary fence and end the hike at the trailhead.

Pundt Park: Pundt Lake, Creekside, Walnut, Red Bay, and Hardwood Trails

Folks who like to explore new trails will not be disappointed with these recent additions to the Spring Creek Greenway that opened in March 2009. Follow a series of well-marked, point-to-point trails around Hart Pundt Lake, along Spring Creek, and through woods filled with walnut and red bay trees. Watch for birds and mammals, including deer and wild pigs.

Start: Hart Pundt Lake trailhead, adjacent to main parking area, by playground

Distance: 2.0-mile loop with a short connecting loop

Approximate hiking time: 1.75 hours

Difficulty: Moderate due to minor elevation changes and uneven trail surface

Trail surface: Mulch, dirt, gravel, asphalt

Seasons: Year-round

Other trail users: Equestrians

Canine compatibility: Leashed dogs permitted

Fees and permits: None required

Schedule: Jan and Dec, 8 a.m.–5 p.m.; Feb and Nov, 8 a.m.–6 p.m.; Mar–Oct, 8 a.m.–7 p.m.

Maps: Trail maps available at the park office; USGS: Maedan

Trail contact: Park Manager, 4164 Spring Creek Dr., Spring 77373; (281) 353-8100; www.hcp4.net/parks/pundt

Other: Restrooms and drinking water, including a doggie fountain, are available at the playground parking area.

Finding the trailhead: From the north side of Houston at the intersection of North Sam Houston Parkway East, merge onto I-45 North. Follow I-45 North for 7 miles and take exit 68 toward Cypresswood Drive. Turn right onto East Cypresswood, proceed 2 miles, and turn left onto Aldine Westfield Road. Go 0.1 mile and turn right onto Spring Creek Drive. Follow Spring Creek Drive for 1.9 miles to the park entrance at 4164 Spring Creek Dr. Check in at the park headquarters at the entrance and then proceed to the playground parking lot. Lock your vehicle. *DeLorme: Texas Atlas & Gazetteer:* Page 71, H12. GPS: N30 4.865' / W95 22.673'

THE HIKE

top at the park office just inside the entrance gate and pick up a trail map, then drive to the playground parking area. Restroom facilities and water fountains are available there. Take water, since no potable water is available on the trail. Use insect repellant and sunscreen, and wear a hat. Start the hike at the Hart Pundt Lake trailhead, next to the kiosk south of the playground parking area. There is a large map of the park on the kiosk. Take the right branch at the trailhead T and then head into the woods. The trail is flat, sand-based, and surfaced with mulch.

The one-acre Hart Pundt Lake quickly comes into view. Follow clockwise around the lake, stopping to go to the water's edge and investigate its creatures. Look for small fish, toads, frogs, pond insects (including dragonflies and water striders), and masses of frog eggs in the spring. There are several wooden benches and a wooden swing around the lake edge. After circling the lake, return to the trailhead and kiosk.

Turn right at the kiosk and head south until reaching the Cross Trail. The trail is sandy and the shade is intermittent. From this point forward there is a series of short point-to-point trails. Each trail is appropriately named for the type of trees along its edges. The trails form an irregular counterclockwise loop that ends at the playground parking area. Navigate through several Ts and a park road while head-

Bald Cypress trees show their knobby roots, near the Spring Creek Greenway Trail.

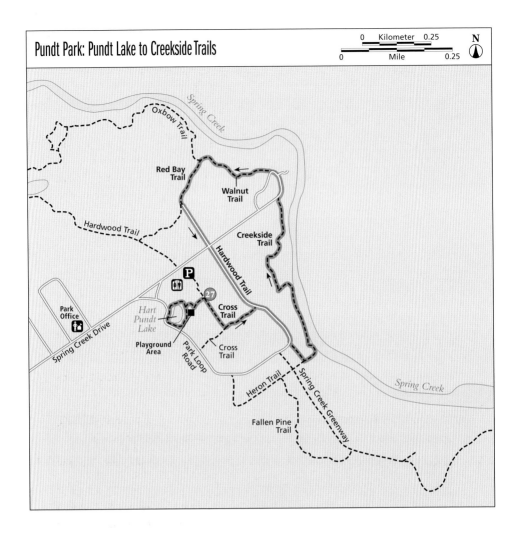

ing south and then east to the T with the Creekside Trail. Head north on the Creekside Trail, which rises gradually. Spring Creek is on the right and comes in and out of sight, depending on the tree cover. Watch for bald cypress trees near the water, with their knobby roots. There is a 15-foot drop-off to the creek. The creek is usually very shallow, but can be unpredictable during heavy rains.

Continue following the trail along the creek in a northerly direction. Pass Spring Creek Drive, which is the park road that allows access to Spring Creek for canoeists. The Creekside Trail ends where it joins the Walnut Trail. Take a hard left and head away from the creek, going northwest. Watch for walnut trees in the woods. In the fall they can be identified by the black crust covering the 1.5-inch-round walnut fruit, either hanging in the trees or lying on the ground. The trail wanders through the woods, and several paths lead to the creek to allow canoe access. Pass by some benches that were built by Eagle Scouts and overlook the creek. This is a good spot to rest and enjoy the solitude before reaching the Y with the Oxbow Trail and Red Bay Trail.

Mixed among the red bay trees are several varieties of oaks. In the fall squirrels may be seen gathering nuts to tide them over the winter. The trail slopes downward and then flattens as it leads into the woods. Reach a T with the Hardwood Trail and take the left branch, heading south. Notice the live oak and walnut trees on each side of the trail. Pass a kiosk that marks the trailhead for the Hardwood Trail. It has a large trail map, so it's easy to see where you've been. Use caution when crossing Spring Creek Drive, and end the hike at the playground parking area.

MILES AND DIRECTIONS

0.0   Start from the kiosk marking the Hart Pundt Lake trailhead. Go right a short distance and then left into the woods. Within 100 yards reach a T. The branches of the T form a loop around the small lake. Take the left branch, heading south around the lake. The lake is on the right. Reach a Y and take the right branch, heading north. The left branch leads to the road.

0.2   Continue around the lake, which is 5 to 10 feet away from the trail's edge. Pass a large wooden swing on the left.

0.3   Reach the Y where the lake loop started and take the left branch, heading east. Follow this short trail until reaching the kiosk at the trailhead.

0.4   After reaching the kiosk turn right, heading south onto the connector trail leading to the Cross Trail.

0.5   Reach a T with the Cross Trail and take the left branch, heading east. Within 200 feet reach a T with a gravel road and turn right, heading south. Follow the road until reaching a T with Heron Trail.

0.7   Turn left and follow Heron Trail until reaching a T with the Creekside Trail. In 250 feet, at the Creekside Trail, take the left branch, heading north. Follow the trail generally north, with Spring Creek on the right (east).

The leaves of the red bay tree are the common bay leaves used to season soups, stews, spaghetti sauce, and other foods.

0.9 Pass the canoe put-in path on the right. Continue following the Creekside Trail, which takes a hard left away from the creek.

1.2 Pass a path on the right that leads to Spring Creek. The path is blocked by a wooden barrier. Continue straight ahead.

1.3 Reach a T with a road and take the right branch, heading north and leading to the Walnut Trail.

1.4 Follow the Walnut Trail, generally northwest, until reaching the T with the Red Bay Trail.

1.8 Follow the Red Bay Trail until reaching a T with the Hardwood Trail. Take the left branch, leading to the parking area near the trailhead. Follow the Hardwood Trail, passing a kiosk with a large park map, and cross the park road.

2.0 End the hike at the playground parking area.

Butterflies

Texas affords hikers a visual pleasure no other state can equal—the abundant, colorful butterflies. They may be seen along the trail or road, or in your backyard. Over 430 species have been recorded across the state, while Arizona, in second place, has only 325 species on record. The opportunity to observe their graceful flights, interrupted by sipping nectar from colorful plants, exists on every trail. Spring and fall are the times of greatest diversity.

Near Houston, the following species are most commonly seen: The easy-to-spot Gulf Fritillary, with a wingspan of over 2.5 inches and orange body, is often mistaken for the monarch. The black swallowtail, another large butterfly, stands out with its black wings that have yellow or white spots. Slightly smaller is the American painted lady, recognized by its orange-brown color and wings showing eyespots. The satyrs with less than a 2-inch wingspan are easy to identify by their gray-brown color and eyespots on their wings. These four butterflies enjoy diverse habitats and, with the exception of the month of January, can be seen throughout the year. Watching for butterflies along a trail can add a dimension to any hike, especially in the hot summer months, when birds are scarce. Take along a guidebook to aid in identification.

Pundt Park: Spring Creek Greenway and Fallen Pine Trail

This hike is for those who like to mix open woods with heavy woods, small ponds, cypress bogs, and cleared resting areas. It is a new trail, having been completed in mid-2009, and is one of the first of a series of connector trails for the Spring Creek Greenway project. Pundt Park is a new park created to facilitate the greenway. The ambitious project will be a hiker's dream, connecting a total of 32 miles of trails along Spring Creek.

Start: Spring Creek Greenway Trail trailhead near end of Park Loop Road

Distance: 2.2-mile loop with an out and back

Approximate hiking time: 1.25 hours

Difficulty: Easy due to flat surface with shade

Trail surface: Mulch, dirt, asphalt

Seasons: Year-round

Other trail users: Dog walkers, equestrians

Canine compatibility: Leashed dogs permitted

Fees and permits: None required

Schedule: Jan and Dec, 8 a.m.–5 p.m.; Feb and Nov, 8 a.m.–6 p.m.; Mar–Oct, 8 a.m.–7 p.m.

Maps: Trail maps available at the park office; USGS: Maedan

Trail contact: Park Manager, 4129 Spring Creek Dr., Spring 77373: (281) 353-4196; www.hcp4.net/parks/pundt

Other: Restroom facilities and drinking water fountains, including a doggie fountain, are available at the playground.

Finding the trailhead: From the north side of Houston at the intersection of North Sam Houston Parkway East, merge onto I-45 North. Follow I-45 North for 7 miles and take exit 68 toward Cypresswood Drive. Turn right onto East Cypresswood, proceed 2 miles, and turn left onto Aldine Westfield Road. Go 0.1 mile and turn right onto Spring Creek Drive. Follow Spring Creek Drive for 1.9 miles to the park entrance at 4164 Spring Creek Dr. Check in at the park headquarters at the entrance and then proceed to the playground parking lot. Lock your vehicle. *DeLorme: Texas Atlas & Gazetteer:* Page 71, H12. GPS: N30 4.754' / W95 22.509'

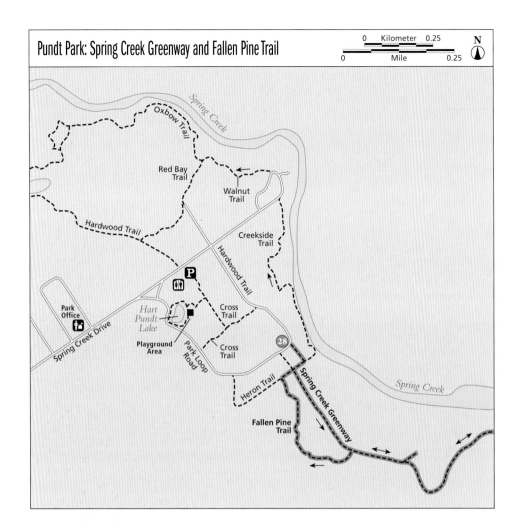

Pundt Park: Spring Creek Greenway and Fallen Pine Trail

THE HIKE

Follow the Park Loop Road to the Spring Creek Greenway kiosk, on the right side of the road. Park off the road, lock your vehicle, and check out the large trail map on the kiosk. The trail is on the left side of the road. It is one of the major connecting trails in the Spring Creek Greenway Project and will eventually lead through Stahl Preserve to Jesse Jones Park. Take water, since there is no potable water along the trail. Wear insect repellant to ward off the mosquitoes found in the swampy areas, and wear a hat and use sunscreen to protect against the Texas sun. As more trails, rest areas, and interpretive sections are added to this 380-acre park, which opened in 2009, it will become one of the crown jewels in the Harris County Precinct 4 park system.

Follow the trail south as it travels between the road and the woods. In less than 0.1 mile, pass the Creekside Trail on the left and the Heron Trail on the right. Watch for inland sea oats along the sides of the trail. The tree canopy is good to intermittent. Spring Creek is to the east, but hidden by trees. There are a few loblolly and short-leaf pines mixed with the hardwoods. The trail is flat, mulched, and varies in width from 3 feet to 6 feet. Veer left just ahead of a large vehicular bridge to explore the Red Bay Sitting Area. Relax on the benches while examining some of the impressive red bay trees. This is especially visually pleasing during the fall when the leaves change color.

Return to the Spring Creek Greenway Trail, turn left, and cross the bridge over Smith Ditch, which flows to Spring Creek. Good photo ops are available from the center of the bridge. Continue following the trail through the woods that now contain mostly loblolly pines. The trail shifts from the left side of the road to the right side, still in the woods. Follow the trail as it circles around five large trees and leads through swampy areas, harboring hungry mosquitoes.

Stop at 1.0 mile and backtrack 0.7 mile to the Fallen Pine Trail, which intersects the Spring Creek Greenway from the left. Take Fallen Pine, which heads west for a short distance and then turns and reaches the Spring Creek Greenway Trail trailhead to end the hike.

A father and daughters stop along the trail to check out the park map.

MILES AND DIRECTIONS

0.0 Start from the kiosk at the Spring Creek Greenway Trail trailhead and head south along the road and into the woods. Within the first 200 feet, pass by the Creekside Trail on the left, where it Ts into the Spring Creek Greenway Trail, and the Heron Trail on the right, where it also Ts into the Spring Creek Greenway Trail. Continue following the trail with the road on the right and woods on the left.

0.4 Reach a trail marker on the left. The path on the left leads to the Red Bay Sitting Area. Take the path to the left and go out and back to the sitting area. Stop here and backtrack to the Spring Creek Greenway Trail and the road.

0.6 Reach the Spring Creek Greenway Trail and turn left, heading south. The trail and road merge where a large concrete bridge crosses Smith Ditch. Cross the bridge and follow the trail, which is on the left side of the road.

0.8 Pass a path on the right that leads into the woods. There is a gully on the left, about 25 feet away.

1.0 Pass a red-lettered sign posted about 10 feet high on a tree that reads CON-SERVATION EASEMENT—ABSOLUTELY NO MOTORIZED VEHICLES. The trail and adjoining road make a loop around a clump of four or five trees. Stop at this point and backtrack over the bridge to where the Fallen Pine Trail inter-sects from the left.

1.8 Reach the Fallen Pine Trail and turn left. Follow the trail, bearing hard right and then back left. Equestrians use this trail.

2.1 Reach a T with the Heron Trail and take the right branch. Follow the Heron Trail until it reaches the park road. Turn left onto the road and follow it back to the trailhead.

2.2 End the hike at the trailhead.

Spring Creek Greenway

Pundt Park, located in Harris County Precinct 4, opened in 2009 as a corner-stone in the Spring Creek Greenway Project. It is the pivotal park connecting the entire 32-mile Spring Creek Greenway trail system, from Jesse Jones Park (Hike 18) in Humble to the southeast and Burroughs Park (Hike 31) in Tomball to the northwest. Commissioner Jerry Eversole hosted a ribbon-cutting cere-mony and grand opening celebration on March 5, 2009, to commemorate the completion of phase I construction of Pundt Park and the first phase of the Spring Creek Greenway. Following the ceremony, guests toured Pundt Park and visited the Carmine Stahl Preserve.

Spring Creek Greenway Trail (Hike 28), a short multiuse trail, is one of two trails in phase 1 of the Spring Creek Greenway trail system. The second trail completed begins at Jesse Jones Park and was named the Judy Overby Bell Trail (Hike 18). It reaches to Stahl Preserve, which is an adjoining 115-acre par-cel that was obtained by Harris County Precinct 4 in 2009. A 7.5-mile trail sec-tion through Stahl Preserve will connect Pundt Park to Jesse Jones Park. The Spring Creek Greenway will provide hikers with lots of leg room.

This hike is for those who love woods, creeks, native plants, and wildlife. The trail winds through the woods past wetlands and ponds. There are overlooks for Spring and Panther Creeks, showing their high sandy banks. Small warblers like the heavy forest understory, while shorebirds, including egrets, enjoy the creeks. Water snakes may be seen from the bridge on the truck access road.

Start: Loop Trail trailhead just south of entrance gate

Distance: 1.7 miles of loops and out and backs

Approximate hiking time: 2 hours

Difficulty: Moderate due to some narrow dirt-surfaced trails

Trail surface: Dirt, sand

Seasons: Year-round

Other trail users: Bird-watchers, dog walkers

Canine compatibility: Leashed dogs permitted

Fees and permits: None required

Schedule: Dawn to dusk

Maps: Trail maps available at the office and the trailhead; USGS: Spring

Trail contact: Montgomery County Preserve, 1130 Pruitt Rd., The Woodlands, 77380; (281) 771-8686; www.pct3.hctx.net/about precinct/parklocations

Other: Restrooms and potable water are located in the preserve office. No potable water or restrooms on the trail.

Finding the trailhead: From north Houston at the intersection of Beltway 8 East and I-45 North, take I-45 North for 12.1 miles. At exit 73 take the Rayford-Sawdust exit and turn left onto Sawdust Road. Follow Sawdust Road west for 1 mile to Budde Road and turn left (south) onto Budde, which turns into Pruitt Road. Follow Pruitt to the Montgomery County Preserve entrance sign and turn right into the parking area at 1118 Pruitt Rd. Turn right into the parking lot adjacent to the park office. Lock your vehicle. *DeLorme: Texas Atlas & Gazetteer:* Page 71, H12. GPS: N30 6.719' / W95 27.109'

THE HIKE

S top at the park office adjacent to the parking area and pick up a park map. If the office is closed, maps are available at the trailhead. The wildflower display in front of the office attracts butterflies, birds, bees, and other critters. Head south from the office and pass through the gate into the 71-acre trail and Spring Creek Greenway area. This section is permanently protected from development by a conservation easement held by the Legacy Land Trust. The Spring Creek Green-

A young couple determines the best way around a muddy stretch of trail. Many trails in the Houston area have muddy spots after a rain.

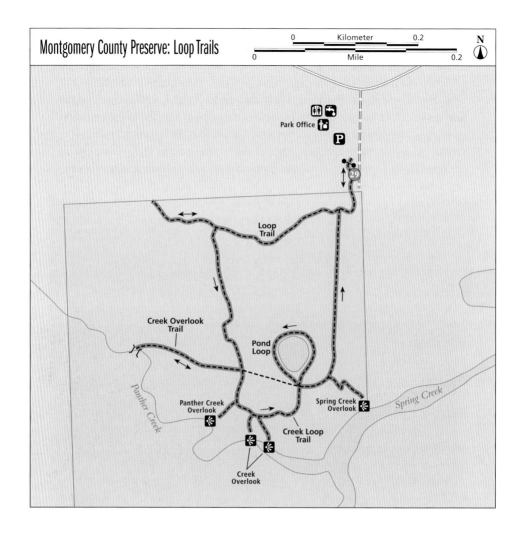

Kilometer

Mile

N

Park Office

Loop
Trail

Creek Overlook
Trail

Pond
Loop

Panther Creek
Overlook

Spring Creek
Overlook

Spring Creek

Panther Creek

Creek Loop
Trail

Creek
Overlook

way will connect 12,000 acres along both sides of Spring Creek, creating over 32 miles of trails. The entire preserve, which was established in 2002, covers 71,400 acres. Bring drinking water, use insect repellant, and wear a hat. Watch for poison ivy, which can be found throughout the preserve.

Head south on the trail, which is narrow and has a dirt surface. A chain-link fence 40 feet away can be seen through the woods. Cross the gravel access road to the Loop Trail trailhead and head west into the woods to walk the loop counterclockwise. There are many downed trees, some from age and others from Hurricane Ike in 2008. The trees have become a prime home to parchment fungi. These polypores are the primary forest recyclers, slowly converting the dying wood into the nutrients needed to nourish growing trees.

Reach the preserve greenway boundary, backtrack to the T, and take the right branch of the Loop Trail south. Pass by a wooden bench constructed by Eagle Scouts from an original Aldo Leopold design. Aldo Leopold (1887–1948), from Wisconsin, is considered the father of wildlife ecology. Do a short out and back to the outdoor classroom on the right side of the trail. The woods contain some loblolly pines and a variety of hardwoods, including American hornbean. This short tree is also known as musclewood, or ironwood. In early spring it has yellow and orange flowers, and in the fall the leaves change from green to orange and yellow.

Continue on the Loop Trail until reaching a T and take the right branch onto a gravel service road. Stop at the bridge over Panther Creek. The creek is down sandy slopes to sand beaches. There are several benches, surrounded by mulberry trees, overlooking the creek. Water snakes, including nonvenomous black-banded water snakes and venomous water moccasins, may be in or around the creek. Backtrack to the T and take the right branch, heading south on the Creek Loop Trail.

The trail is narrow and sometimes overgrown. At the end of the trail, an opening creates an overlook down to Panther Creek. Back-track to a Y and take the right branch, heading southeast. This is a branch of the Creek Loop Trail and leads to another creek overlook. Backtrack and bear right, heading east and then north on the Creek Loop Trail. Notice the hard-woods, including water oak, post oak, sycamore, and southern magnolia. Cross the service road to the Pond Loop trailhead.

This wetland pond depends on rain and runoff water to fill it. This area is a favorite hangout for dragonflies, and swamp rabbits have been seen near the pond. The several benches around the pond and the signage are the projects of Eagle Scouts. Black willow and bald cypress trees grow by the edge of the pond, and a clump of bamboo is on the west side. This native bamboo is commonly called river cane, and the green-colored trunks are only a half inch in diameter. Dwarf palmettos, scattered in the woods, are known as the indicator species for wetlands.

Go a short distance east on the service road. Take the right to Spring Creek Over-look, then return to the road. Turn right (north) to finish the hike. Woods are on both sides of the road, but there is no shade. Notice the patches of Japanese climbing fern. This plant is an extremely aggressive invasive that climbs around and chokes out local plants. These trails are great to hike during different seasons, as they present constantly changing colors, bird species, and plants.

MILES AND DIRECTIONS

0.0 Start from the Loop Trail trailhead just south of the entrance gate and across the gravel access road.

0.1 Pass a wooden bench on the left and continue following the trail.

0.3 Reach a T and take the right branch, heading west. Continue on the trail until reaching a chain-link fence, which marks the boundary of the conservation easement. Park soccer fields are beyond the fence. Backtrack to the T.

0.4 Reach the T and take the right branch, heading south onto the Loop Trail.

0.5 Pass a wooden bench on the left and then bear right over a dry wash. A path comes in from the right. Turn right off the trail for a short out and back to an outdoor classroom. Backtrack to the Loop Trail.

0.6 Reach the Loop Trail and turn right, heading south. Follow the trail and soon cross the access road to reach the trailhead for the Creek Loop Trail. Continue south on the trail toward Panther Creek.

0.7 Pass two benches on the left and reach a T. Take the right branch heading north/northwest, which is the Creek Overlook Trail, a short out and back to Panther Creek. Backtrack to the T and continue.

1.0 Reach a Y and take the right branch that leads to another creek overlook. Bear left as the trail undulates up and down. Reach the overlook, backtrack to the Y, and take the right branch.

1.1 Cross the gravel access road and reach the trailhead for the Pond Loop Trail. Follow the trail north, then west, then south in a circle around the pond, keeping the pond on the left.

1.3 Reach the service road and turn left, heading for Spring Creek Overlook.

1.4 Bend right to reach the Spring Creek Overlook. Then backtrack to the road.

1.5 Reach the service road and turn right, heading east. Then follow the service road, making a hard left (north) back to the trailhead.

1.7 End the hike back at the trailhead.

The Legacy Land Trust

Montgomery County Preserve (Hike 29) and Little Cypress Creek Preserve (Hike 26) were the first two parks established on property rights acquired by the Legacy Land Trust. The trails in the 71-acre Montgomery County Preserve are a link in the Spring Creek Greenway. The preserve was the first conservation easement in Texas signed with a county government. Little Cypress Creek Preserve contains 60 acres. Both preserves are staffed by employees of the Legacy Land Trust and are permanently protected from commercial development through conservation easements.

In 1996 the Legacy Land Trust was established as an offshoot of the Bayou Preservation Association, a Houston organization whose purpose is to protect the bayou systems and the quality of water that flows into them. The mission of the Legacy Land Trust, a nonprofit organization, is to protect as much as possible the remaining open space surrounding these bayous. Lands having natural appeal or recreational, scenic, or historical value are particularly sought. The Legacy Land Trust, operating in the Greater Houston area, is one of nearly 1,300 land trusts throughout the United States, 30 of which are in Texas. Most of these trusts operate in a specific geographic area, attempting to protect the natural spaces in their region.

Much of the work of the Legacy Land Trust consists of evaluating potential sites and then working with the existing landowners. This requires fieldwork and time-consuming legal work. The culmination of this work is a land preservation agreement with a willing landowner. The owner agrees to permanently set aside his or her property from commercial development and allow it to remain in its natural state. These are voluntary agreements between the landowner and Legacy Land Trust. The landowner retains title to the property and may receive tax benefits from the government. These agreements are win-win situations that benefit the property owner and the public. The current fruits of the Legacy Land Trust are two great hiking areas. The folks at the Legacy Land Trust invite you to come out to enjoy the low-impact activities at these public preserves.

George Mitchell Preserve: Nature Loop Trail

This hike offers a creek, dense woods, birds, and wildlife, including deer. The preserve is conveniently located on the south side of The Woodlands, north of Houston. Although surrounded by bustling subdivisions, this 1,700-acre preserve provides a pleasant getaway. The trail opened in the spring of 2008 and is a major link in the Spring Creek Greenway Project, which will allow hikers access to 32 miles of connected trails.

Start: Nature Trail trailhead adjacent to preserve parking area
Distance: 2.2-mile lollipop
Approximate hiking time: 1.5 hours
Difficulty: Easy due to flat trails and shade
Trail surface: Dirt, sand
Seasons: Year-round
Other trail users: Dog walkers
Canine compatibility: Leashed dogs permitted
Fees and permits: None required

Schedule: Dawn to dusk
Maps: Trail map available at www.springcreekgreenway.org; USGS: Oklahoma
Trail contact: Montgomery County Precinct 3, 1130 Pruit Rd., Spring 77380; (281) 367-3977; www.springcreekgreenway.com
Other: No potable water or restrooms on the trail. Print out a trail map from the Web site.

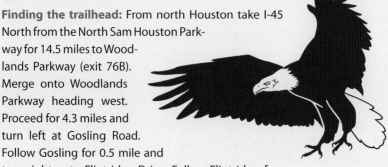

Finding the trailhead: From north Houston take I-45 North from the North Sam Houston Parkway for 14.5 miles to Woodlands Parkway (exit 76B). Merge onto Woodlands Parkway heading west. Proceed for 4.3 miles and turn left at Gosling Road. Follow Gosling for 0.5 mile and turn right onto Flintridge Drive. Follow Flintridge for 0.5 mile to 5171 Flintridge Dr. and the George Mitchell Preserve signs. Turn into the small parking area. Lock your vehicle. *DeLorme: Texas Atlas & Gazetteer:* Page 71, G11. GPS: N30 9.762' / W95 31.080'

S tart at the Nature Loop Trail trailhead, adjacent to the parking area. The signage is very good. Bring drinking water since none is available on the trail, and use insect repellant to ward off attacking mosquitoes. The trail is 6 feet wide and mostly gravel. A short connector trail leads to the Nature Loop Trail. This trail is part of a series of connector parks and trails that form the Spring Creek Greenway, which, when finished, will form a 32-mile continuous linear trail along Spring Creek—a bonanza for hikers.

At the Y, which connects both ends of the loop, take the right branch, heading west. Watch for a bike trail that intersects from the left. Your trail goes through the woods, which has a mix of hardwoods and loblolly pines. The woods, combined with some wetlands and Spring Creek, provide excellent habitat for birds and mammals. Watch for white-tailed deer, raccoon, and armadillo tracks in sandy sections of the trail. Raccoon tracks are numerous and easy to identify. They look much like a human hand, with five digits. They are 2 to 4 inches long, and their walking stride is 8 to 18 inches. The trail is marked with 4-foot-tall 6-by-6 marker posts.

The understory of the woods contains shrubs and small trees, including American beautyberry. Look for old rotting logs along the trail's edge, which furnish good photo ops. They provide nourishment for toadstools and other colorful

The area around Bedias Lake appears to be semi-tropical with its heavy growth of ferns and other plants.

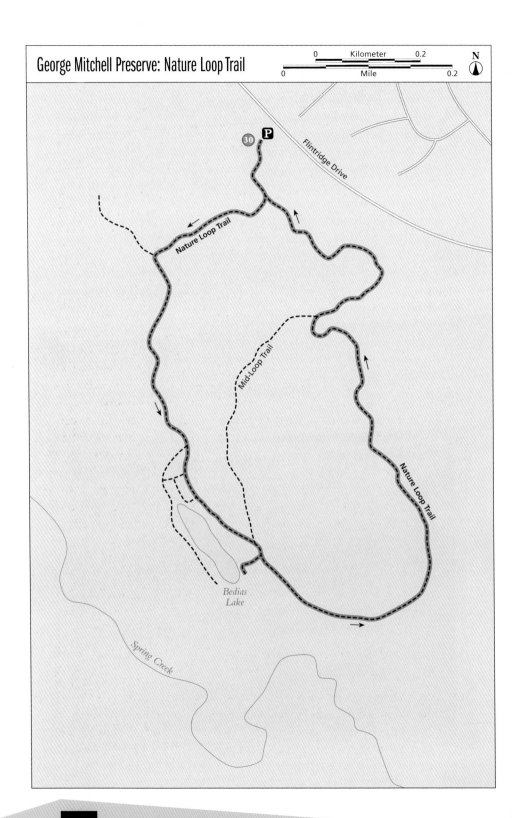

George Mitchell Preserve: Nature Loop Trail

Kilometer
0   0.2
Mile
0   0.2

N

30 P

Flintridge Drive

Nature Loop Trail

Mid-Loop Trail

Nature Loop Trail

Bedias
Lake

Spring Creek

fungi. A large number of trees were downed by Hurricane Ike in 2008 and will feed the forest floor for many years to come. Some of the uprooted tree roots cling to their ball of earth. A number of ferns have begun to colonize in some open areas.

About 0.8 mile into the hike, reach a Y. Take the right branch that leads to Bedias Lake. This is a small lake west of the Nature Loop Trail. Follow along the edge of the lake, listening and watching for birds and small mammals. Backtrack to the Nature Trail and continue following it.

Reach an inverted Y at 0.9 mile. The left branch is the connection with the Mid-Loop Trail. It crosses from the east side to the west side of the Nature Loop Trail. The Mid-Loop Trail branch may be taken to shorten the hike. Continue on the right branch. The trail becomes a little sandy and narrow. There is a short out and back called the Creek View Trail that is an interesting walk along the edge of the creek. Sometimes the low-hanging tree branches form an arch over the trail.

Watch for colorful wildflowers, including varieties of sunflowers and morning glories, during the spring and fall. The woods generally reach to the trail's edge, with only a few openings. The tree canopy ranges from good to intermittent. Listen and watch for low-flying birds flitting in and out of the woods. During the spring migration, many species of warblers may be identified, including the ruby-crowned kinglet. They travel in small groups and winter in Texas. Continue following the Nature Loop Trail as it squiggles a little from the right to the left and back.

Follow the Nature Loop Trail and watch for numerous bike paths that generally intersect from the left. Reach the Y where the ends of the Nature Loop Trail join. Take the right branch, which is marked by an exit sign, and backtrack on the connector trail to the trailhead.

The preserve was named for George Mitchell, founder of The Woodlands community. He is a native Texan and founded Mitchell Energy and Development in 1946. Mitchell has been a generous contributor to many nature-related projects.

MILES AND DIRECTIONS

0.0   Start from the Nature Trail trailhead adjacent to the parking area. After 200 feet reach a T and take the left branch, heading east. In another 200 feet reach a Y and take the right branch. Pass a bike path on the left.

0.2   Pass a trail marker post and then reach a Y. Take the left branch and bear left.

0.5   Continue to follow the trail as it ambles right and left. Reach a Y and take the left branch, following the loop. The right branch leads more directly to Bedias Lake. We'll get there by following the loop. Continue through the woods, with the creek overflow on the right.

0.8   Reach a path intersecting from the right, leading down to Bedias Lake. Take the path to investigate the water and return to the main trail. This is an alternate route to Bedias Lake. At the main trail, turn right.

0.9   Pass a marker post and reach an inverted Y. Take the right branch, following the loop. The left branch is the Mid-Loop Trail. This is a shortcut across the loop and may be taken to shorten the hike.

1.0   Pass a marker post showing the Nature Loop Trail to the left and the Creek View Trail to the right. Continue going straight on the main trail. The path to the right, the Creek View Trail, is a short out and back down to the creek.

1.2   Pass a marker post showing a path to the wetlands on the right. Continue going straight on the main trail.

1.3   Continue following the main trail as it bears right and left. Pass several bike paths intersecting the main trail from the left.

1.7   Pass a marker post stating NO RIGHT TURN. A small path leads to the right. Stay on the main trail. From the marker post, follow the trail bearing right, then hard left, and then straight ahead.

1.8   Reach a Y and take the right branch. The left branch is the end of the Mid-Loop Trail that was passed at 0.9 mile.

1.9   Continue following the Nature Loop Trail, bearing right and left until reaching a Y. Take the left branch toward the trailhead.

2.0   Pass a marker post and then reach a Y. Take the right branch, marked EXIT. The left branch is a bike trail. Within 200 feet reach a Y. Take the right branch and backtrack to the trailhead. This is the point where the loop was started.

2.2   End the hike at the trailhead.

Burroughs Park: Nature and Lake Trails

Experience the solitude of trails winding through woods, with the opportunity to see many species of birds and other wildlife. Deer, armadillos, and snakes all reside here. Watch for red-bellied woodpeckers, pine warblers, and white egrets. Circle around a three-acre fishing lake that boasts a beaver lodge. This is a good adventure for young children. This 320-acre park is located in Tomball, about 20 miles northwest of Houston.

Start: Nature Trail trailhead adjacent to north parking area

Distance: 1.5 miles of interconnecting loops

Approximate hiking time: 1.25 hours

Difficulty: Moderate due to a sandy section of trail and short up-and-down slopes

Trail surface: Crushed granite, dirt, sand, asphalt

Seasons: Best Sept–June

Other trail users: Dog walkers

Canine compatibility: Leashed dogs permitted

Fees and permits: None required

Schedule: 7 a.m.–dark

Maps: None available in the park; trail map available at www.hcp4.net/Parks/burroughs; USGS: Oklahoma

Trail contact: Burroughs Park Manager, 9738 Hufsmith Rd., Tomball 77375; (281) 353-4196; www.hcp4.net/parks/burroughs

Other: Restrooms and water fountains are located in a concrete block building near the trailhead. Water fountains are also available in the playground area.

Finding the trailhead: From north Houston at the intersection of I-45 North and North Sam Houston Parkway East, merge onto I-45 North. Continue on I-45 North for 7.8 miles and take exit 70A toward FM 2920 and Tomball. After 1.3 miles turn left onto Spring Cypress Road. Continue straight for 0.5 mile to FM 2920. Turn left onto FM 2920. After 4.3 miles make a slight turn right onto Kuykendahl Road. Follow Kuykendahl for 4.9 miles and turn left onto Hufsmith Road. Follow Hufsmith for 1.2 miles to the Burroughs Park entrance at 9738 Hufsmith Rd. Follow the park road to the last parking area near the restrooms and pavilion. *DeLorme: Texas Atlas & Gazetteer:* Page 71, H11. GPS: N30 8.296' / W95 34.568'

THE HIKE

Start at the Nature Trail trailhead adjacent to the north parking area. There is a map board at the trailhead that was constructed by Eagle Scouts. Turn left, heading west into the woods around the Nature Loop. The trail surface is crushed granite and 7 feet wide. The mosquitoes can be troublesome, so use insect repellant. The first mile of the trail has excellent tree canopy, furnishing shade.

The woods are a mix of loblolly pines and hardwoods, including hickory and oak. There are still some downed trees from Hurricane Ike in 2008. Unless the trees present a hazard, the park department allows them to decay naturally. Some portions along the trail's edge have been cleared, creating an opportunity to see birds and possibly some deer. Watch and listen for red-bellied woodpeckers. Seeing the small patch of red on their belly can be difficult, but their red crown and black and white zebra stripes down their back make this robin-size bird easy to identify.

At the first T take the right branch, heading north, and in less than 300 feet reach another T and take the right branch. Follow the trail, which is mostly sand, until reaching the top of a low hill. Since the area is semiopen, this is a good spot to watch for butterflies. In the summer months after a rain, swallowtails, a medium-size butterfly, may be seen gathering around mud puddles. Stay on the trail because the woods can have copperhead snakes, a venomous but normally not aggressive species that lives here.

Reach a T that has both branches bordered by a natural gas pipeline and barbed-wire fence. Take the right branch, with the fence on the left. The trail surface transitions from sand to hard dirt, making walking easier. Within 100 feet reach a Y and continue straight, taking the left branch. The barbed-wire fence is still on the left, and heavy woods are on the right. Go down a steep slope and break out into an opening. There is a T, with both branches being asphalt. Take the left branch, which has heavy woods on the left and the lake on the right.

This starts the Lake Trail that loops around the three-acre lake. The area around the lake is mowed and has picnic tables. Pass a bench on the right and then cross a wooden bridge. Watch for egrets (a large white bird) and other shorebirds around the lake. Dragonflies will be hovering near the water, looking for a meal of mosquitoes. They are a hiker's friend in reducing the mosquito population. Their wingspan is about 4 inches, and their bodies many be red, green, or yellow. Some folks may remember when their grandmother told them to keep away from dragonflies because they could stitch your mouth closed. (It's not true!)

A beaver can cut down a 3-inch tree in ten minutes.
The trees are then used to build a dam and lodge.

Look for a beaver lodge just before the trail curves to the west. This is a favorite fishing spot for the shorebirds and provides good photo ops. There are benches available, making this a good place to rest and enjoy the activities. Turtles bask on any piece of floating log. Some state record trees are on the west side of the lake, including an 85-foot-high winged elm. Continue following the asphalt trail around the lake and past the playground and a maze made from shrubs. Cross the parking lot and go back to the trailhead.

The Texas Parks & Wildlife Department stocks the lake with trout during January. This draws crowds of avid anglers and makes the park more crowded than normal.

MILES AND DIRECTIONS

0.0 Start from the Nature Trail trailhead adjacent to the north side of the last parking area. Turn left and head west into the woods.

0.2 Follow the trail straight ahead, then bear right, heading north. In 250 feet, reach a T and take the right branch, heading northeast. The left branch leads to several miles of primitive trails.

A white egret takes off from the lake in Burroughs Park. Other shorebirds and warblers can be seen most of the year. The lake also has a beaver lodge.

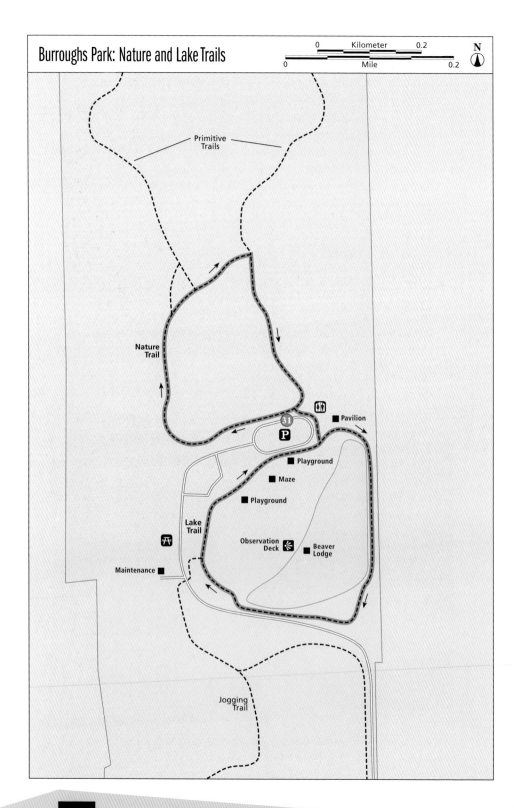

Burroughs Park: Nature and Lake Trails

Primitive
Trails

Nature
Trail

Pavilion

31 P

Playground

Maze

Playground

Lake
Trail

Observation
Deck

Beaver
Lodge

Maintenance

Jogging
Trail

N

0   Kilometer   0.2

0   Mile   0.2

0.4 Continue northeast until reaching a T. Take the right branch, heading south up a minor slope. The left branch leads to those primitive trails again.

0.5 Reach the top of a small hill. The trail is 3- to 5-inch-deep sand. Continue heading south and pass a path that leads out of the woods on the right.

0.6 Reach a T with a natural gas pipeline and barbed-wire fence straight ahead. Take the right branch, with the fence on the left. Follow the trail about 100 feet and reach a Y. Take the left branch, heading south.

0.7 Break out from the woods into the open. Reach a T, where the trail surface changes to asphalt. This ends the Nature Trail and begins the Lake Trail. The lake is straight ahead. Take the left branch, heading east, and then bear right, following the shoreline of the lake. Woods are on the left.

0.9 Follow the trail south, with the lake on the right. At the end of the lake, bear hard right, going west.

1.1 The trail bends right, heading north, with the lake on the right and the park road on the left. Pass the park maintenance building on the left.

1.3 Pass a path on the right leading to a playground and a path on the left leading to a parking area. Continue bearing to the right. There is a drinking fountain on the right. Pass an asphalt path on the right that leads to a shrubbery maze. Continue on the Lake Trail, heading northeast. A playground and boardwalk are on the right.

1.4 Continue and cross a parking area to return to the Nature Trail trailhead.

1.5 End the hike back at the trailhead.

32 Kleb Woods Nature Preserve: Farm, Wetlands, and Nature Center Trails

Pass by a remnant prairie on the Nature Center Trail and then follow the Farm Trail Loop that leads past early twentieth-century buildings from the Kleb homestead. The Wetlands Trail goes through woods containing loblolly pine, eastern red cedar, live oak, and other hardwoods. A boardwalk crosses patches of wetlands. Watch for animals and snakes. Several ponds and an old windmill add additional interest to the hike.

Start: Nature Center Trail trailhead at south edge of parking area
Distance: 1.7 miles of interconnecting loops with an out and back
Approximate hiking time: 1.5 hours
Difficulty: Easy due to flat terrain and good tree cover
Trail surface: Packed gravel, dirt, boardwalks
Seasons: Year-round
Other trail users: Dog walkers, bird-watchers, school groups

Canine compatibility: Leashed dogs permitted
Fees and permits: None required
Schedule: 7 a.m.–dusk
Maps: Trail maps available at the Nature Center; USGS: Rose Hill
Trail contact: Park Manager, 20301 Mueschke Rd., Tomball 77377; (281) 357-5324; www.pct3 .hctx.net/parks/klebwoods naturepres.aspx

Finding the trailhead: From northwest Houston at the Beltway 8 and I-290 intersection, head west on I-290 for 12.3 miles to the Mueschke Road exit. Turn right onto Mueschke Road and travel 6.8 miles to Draper Road and turn left. There is a sign for Kleb Woods on Mueschke Road. The paved parking area is on the left by the Harris County Precinct 3 sign. Lock your vehicle. *DeLorme: Texas Atlas & Gazetteer:* Page 71, H11. GPS: N30 4.319' / W95 44.387

THE HIKE

Start at the Nature Center Trail trailhead on the south side of the parking area. In 2009 there was little trail signage, but there are ongoing projects to develop signage and construct more boardwalks. Use insect repellant to discourage the mosquitoes and other pesky insects, and apply sunscreen because the tree canopy and shade are intermittent.

The Nature Center Trail is a 10-foot-wide gravel road leading to the Nature Center. Seniors and physically disadvantaged folks may use the road to drive their vehicles to the Nature Center. The trail passes through woods and the remnants of a prairie. In years past, prairies were dominant in this area. Plant ID and information markers, 6 to 8 inches high, highlight interesting features. One of the more intriguing signs warns of a roadrunner crossing. This bird, made famous by the Wiley Coyote cartoon series ("beep beep!") is worth looking for because it is usually found farther west.

Reach the Nature Center, which is on the left, and stop to pick up a trail map and birding checklist. With over 200 species of birds, the preserve is a bird-watching hot spot. In the spring watch for sulphur moths and black swallowtail butterflies. Try to identify the birds in the area that are looking for the moths and butterflies

The Wetlands Trail in Kleb Woods winds it way around interesting swamp areas. Several boardwalks help get over the wet ground.

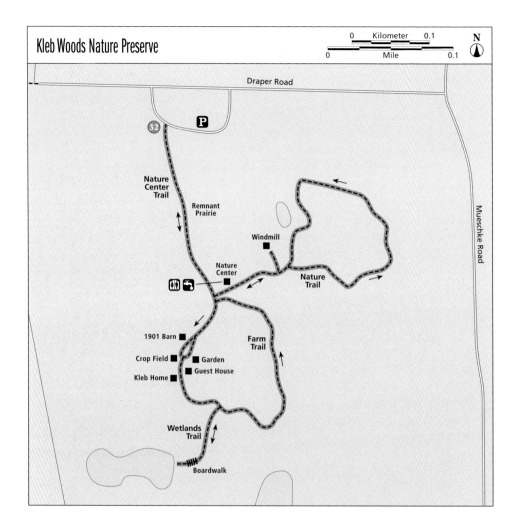

to supplement their diet. Also check out the charismatic picture of Elmer Kleb, for whom the preserve was named. In the rear of the Nature Center is a butterfly garden and benches,

The Farm Trail trailhead is just south of the Nature Center. This trail is a loop, but has been combined with the Wetlands Trail. Follow the 8-foot-wide packed gravel trail as it meanders right and left toward the farm buildings. Watch for screech owl nest boxes placed about 30 to 40 feet up in hardwood trees. Reach the restored Kleb home, guest house, barn, and small garden. Benches and chairs are conveniently placed around this area. An informational sign tells the story of Elmer Kleb. This is a great place to kick back and enjoy.

The Wetlands Trail trailhead is just south of the Kleb home. Head south into the woods on this 5-foot-wide dirt trail. The tree cover is good, furnishing welcome shade during the summer. The area is lowland and can be swampy. A long board-walk, curving right and then left, provides dry walking. Deer frequent this area as well as many varieties of birds and snakes. Nonvenomous rat snakes and black-banded water snakes and venomous water moccasins roam these wetlands. Water oak trees thrive in the swamps, and yaupon dominates the understory. Although yaupon is an invasive species, destroying local plants and habitat, it is a favorite of wrens, robins, and waxwings for nesting sites.

A second boardwalk leads to a seasonal pond, at which point it is necessary to backtrack a short distance. Reach a T that joins the Farm Trail. Take the right branch, heading east and then north. Loblolly pines dominate the woods, but eastern red cedar, Shumard oak, live oak, pecan, and sugarberry are also present. Sugarberry is especially noticeable in the fall, when its green leaves turn to red. Listen for the Carolina chickadee, a small black-headed bird. The chickadee feeds in trees and is rarely seen on the ground, but announces its location with a fast, high-pitched *chic-a-dee-dee-dee-dee* song.

After following the trail back to the Nature Center, go to the Nature Trail trail-head. Take the right branch of this loop and head east into the woods. Pass American beautyberry bushes that have small clusters of bluish flowers from June to August and small, bright purple berries from August to November. These berries are a favorite fruit of birds and animals. In a short distance reach the Windmill Path intersecting the trail from the left. Take the path to the windmill, which presents a good photo op, then return to the Nature Trail, taking the right branch of the Y. Follow the trail through the woods as it forms a loop east, north, and south. At the end of the loop, backtrack past the windmill and to the Nature Center. Backtrack from the Nature Center on the Nature Center Trail to the trailhead and parking area.

MILES AND DIRECTIONS

0.0 Start from the Nature Center Trail trailhead at the south edge of the parking area off Draper Road and head south.

0.1 Reach the Nature Center on the left (east) and proceed to the back, where the Farm Trail trailhead is located.

0.3 Follow the Farm Trail south until reaching the Kleb home, guest house, barn, and garden. Go around the farm buildings until reaching the Wetlands Trail trailhead. Follow the trail into the woods.

0.5 Reach a long boardwalk over a swampy area.

0.7 Reach the end of the boardwalk and immediately bear right, heading toward a large pond. Dead-end at the pond and backtrack to the Y at the end of the boardwalk. Take the right branch.

0.8 Continue following the trail until reaching another boardwalk. In the middle of the boardwalk, exit the boardwalk to a connector trail on the left, then take a hard right into the woods.

0.9 Follow the trail until reaching a T. Take the right branch, heading east and then north, and immediately bear left. The right branch goes to a pasture.

1.0 Come to a small clearing on the left, about 125 feet deep. Bear left, making a small semicircle around the clearing.

1.1 Reach the Nature Center and bear right to the rear of the center to reach the Nature Trail trailhead. The trailhead is at the edge of the woods, opposite the back stairs of the Nature Center.

1.2 Take the path on the left, leading to the windmill. This is a short out-and-back hike. Backtrack to the T intersection with the Nature Trail and take the left branch, heading northeast.

1.3 Reach a T for the Nature Trail loop. Take the right branch, heading east, and walk the loop counterclockwise.

1.5 At the Y closing the loop, turn right (southwest) and retrace your steps past the windmill path to the Nature Center.

1.6 Follow the trail to the Nature Center. From there, backtrack on the Nature Center Trail to the trailhead.

1.7 End the hike back at the trailhead.

Elmer "Lumpy" Kleb

Today, Elmer Kleb (1907–1999), for whom the Kleb Woods Nature Preserve was named, might be called a minimalist, or an extremely stubborn conservationist. In his lifetime he was called other names, including hermit and recluse. Conrad Kleb, a German immigrant and Elmer's grandfather, settled in the 1840s near what became Tomball. The house that Elmer lived in for ninety-two years was built by his father, Edward. Elmer never married and had no children. The Kleb home, guest house, and barn have been restored and are located on the Farm Trail in the preserve.

Some of the folks in Tomball still remember Elmer. He would walk to town, a distance of several miles, to purchase a few needed supplies. He was easy to recognize, with his full gray beard, a knapsack tossed over his shoulder, very bowed legs, and a limp. The limp was caused by an injury and earned him the nickname "Lumpy."

When his parents died, Elmer inherited the farm. However, even though he came from generations of farmers, he never farmed it, but let it revert to woods. He truly enjoyed the company of birds and small animals. Life was simple—just enjoying the land and wildlife and planting some trees and a small garden. He even cared for a few of his wildlife companions in his frugal home, nursing those that were injured back to health. The story goes that

he cared for an injured vulture, who then shared the house. The home was indeed Spartan—no electricity, no phone, and no city water. Living off the land was a satisfying task.

It was as though Elmer and the land, with its flora and fauna, were inseparable. His desires were minimal, just wanting to live on the land that had been owned by his family since the 1840s. He asked no one for anything. There was just one problem, however, which Elmer completely ignored: the tax man. Elmer's mindset was that he owned the land—the government gave him nothing, so why should he have to pay taxes to the government? Over his lifetime the taxes, along with compounding penalties, grew to a very large amount of money. The taxing authorities were considering a forced sale to settle the bill.

Elmer's situation began to attract a lot of attention, including that of Judge Jim Scanlan. The judge placed the property in receivership and appointed an attorney to manage Elmer's finances. The farm was valued at considerably more than the outstanding taxes. The Harris County commissioner for Precinct 3 then became interested in the property to develop as a nature preserve. A group of agencies and individuals, including the Texas Parks & Wildlife Department and the Trust for Public Land, worked with the Precinct 3 commissioner and Elmer's attorney/guardian to secure funds to buy the farm. The tax debt was satisfied, and a trust fund was established to care for Elmer for the rest of his life. He was also allowed to remain in the family home, where he lived until his death in 1999, at the age of 92.

Jones Forest: Sweetleaf Nature Trail

On this short interpretive trail, go past a colony of red-cockaded woodpeckers, an endangered species. Investigate 60 informational signs telling about the plants, trees, and environment. Cross over several bridges, including a suspension bridge. The lush woods offer solitude as the trail traverses the north and south sides of the Rice Branch of an unnamed seasonal creek. The state-champion common sweetleaf tree, from which the trail gets its name, is located near the trail.

Start: Sweetleaf Nature Trail trailhead adjacent to parking area
Distance: 1-mile narrow loop
Approximate hiking time: 1 hour
Difficulty: Easy due to level trail and good tree cover
Trail surface: Dirt, sand
Seasons: Year-round
Other trail users: Bird-watchers
Canine compatibility: Dogs not permitted
Fees and permits: None required
Schedule: Dawn to dusk
Maps: Trail maps available at the park office; USGS: Tamina

Trail contact: Jones Forest Manager, 1328 FM 1488, Conroe 77384; (936) 273-2261; www .stateparks.com/w_g_jones.html
Special considerations: Call the office (936-273-2261) to obtain the combination to the gate lock to enter Nature Trail Road to the Sweetleaf Nature Trail parking area. Be sure to lock the gate after you enter. Lock your vehicle.
Other: Toilet facilities available in the park office. No potable water available on the trail. No bicycles allowed on the trail.

Finding the trailhead: From north Houston at the intersection of I-45 and North Sam Houston Parkway East, merge onto I-45 heading north. Follow I-45 North for 19.8 miles to exit 81. Take exit 81 toward FM 1488. Continue for 0.7 mile. Take the FM 1488 ramp, going slightly right onto FM 1488. Follow FM 1488 to the park headquarters at 1328 FM 1488. Check in with the ranger and get directions to the Sweetleaf Nature Trail and the combination for the lock at the gate. *DeLorme: Texas Atlas & Gazetteer:* Page 71, F11. GPS: N30 14.148' / W95 29.931'

THE HIKE

Pick up a map and interpretive trail guide at the park office and drive about 1 mile west on FM 1488 to the parking area at the Sweetleaf Nature Trail. This forest has 1,733 acres, but there are relatively few trails, since most of the acreage is used as a demonstration and working forest. The forest is on both the north and south sides of FM 1488. Wear sturdy walking shoes, since tree roots reach into the surface. Use insect repellant to discourage the numerous mosquitoes. This

The Sweetleaf Nature Trail follows along a prime section of the endangered, red-cockaded woodpecker's habitat. Spring is the best time to watch for these birds.

is a very short hike but offers many interesting features, including the possibility of seeing the red-cockaded woodpecker, an endangered species.

Start at the trailhead adjacent to the parking area, then head north on a grassy single-lane jeep road. Reach the Y, which begins the loop. Take the left branch and cross Flat Car Bridge over the Rice Branch of an unnamed creek. The creek is about 6 feet below the bridge and, depending on the amount of recent rainfall, may be 6 feet wide and 1 foot deep. The creek crossing furnishes a good photo op. There is a wooden bench on the right and a barbed-wire boundary fence on the left. Starting the hike at the north side of the loop keeps the interpretive markers in order. Follow into the woods and watch for the interpretive signs and markers. Keep your interpretive guide handy to help identify trees and other features that add an extra dimension to the hike.

The trail is flat but has numerous tree roots growing across it. Watch your footing to avoid turning an ankle. The woods are predominantly pines mixed with hickories, elms, oaks, and southern magnolias. Benches are placed at convenient intervals along the trail's edge. At 0.4 mile notice the stark difference between the left and right sides of the trail. On the left is the forester-maintained habitat for the red-cockaded woodpecker. Sections of this area require periodic burning and clearing to remove portions of the understory. This makes it more difficult for predators such as flying squirrels and snakes to reach the birds' nests. It also allows hikers to get a clear view into the nesting area where the woodpeckers build their nests in living pine trees, about 40 feet off the ground. The right side of the trail is heavily wooded and better habitat for deer and other mammals.

Continue following the trail east and pass a bench and sign on the left. The sign tells about trees on the trail and how to identify their leaves. Pass interpretive marker 8 and follow the trail as it bears left and right going east. The creek is about 6 feet away, on the right side of the trail. The red-cockaded woodpecker habitat is still on the left. Reach a Y and take the right branch, going down a slope and then crossing the creek on a suspension bridge that was constructed by Eagle Scouts. Immediately reach a Y and take the right branch, heading west. The red-cockaded woodpecker habitat ended near the bridge. The creek is about 25 feet away, down a slope to the right.

Look for American beautyberry bushes and small ferns. At interpretive marker 50, notice that the heavy canopy has prevented sunlight from reaching the forest floor. With the lack of sunlight, few shrubs and small trees can survive. Cross several bridges over shallow gullies. The creek continues to be on the right, sometimes visible and sometimes obscured by the woods. Reach the T near the Flat Car Bridge and take the left branch back to the trailhead.

Because Jones State Forest has a significant population of endangered red-cockaded woodpeckers, the site has been designated "significant for bird conservation" and a "globally important bird area." Jones Forest and its red-cockaded woodpeckers draw visitors from around the world.

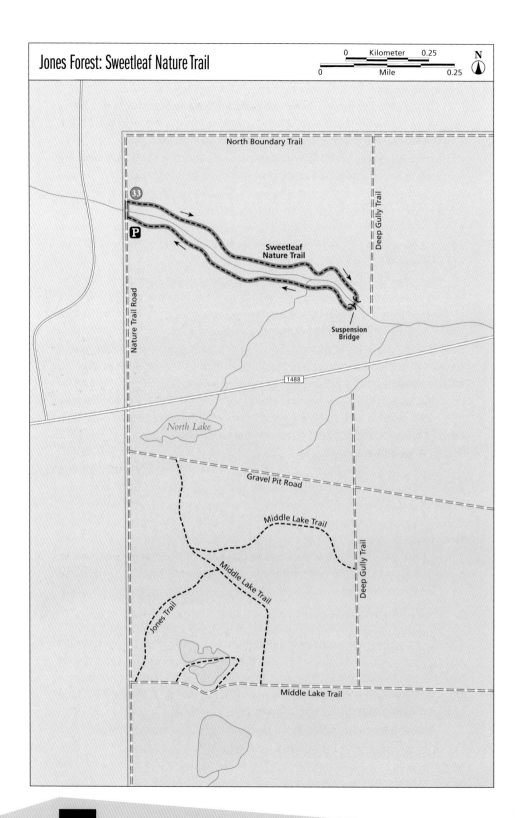

0   Kilometer   0.25

0   Mile   0.25

N

North Boundary Trail

Deep Gully Trail

33

P

Sweetleaf
Nature Trail

Nature Trail Road

Suspension
Bridge

1488

North Lake

Gravel Pit Road

Middle Lake Trail

Deep Gully Trail

Middle Lake Trail

Jones Trail

Middle Lake Trail

MILES AND DIRECTIONS

0.0 Start from the Sweetleaf Nature Trail trailhead, adjacent to the parking area. Head north on the grass road. In 100 yards reach the Y ahead of the Flat Car Bridge. Take the left branch, heading north, and cross the bridge. Bear right at the end of the bridge. This begins the narrow loop, heading east and then west around the Rice Branch of an unnamed creek.

0.2 Pass interpretive markers 1 and 2 on the left. Continue following the trail east.

0.3 Pass interpretive marker 4 on the left and marker 5, water oak, on the right. Bear slightly right and continue following the trail.

0.4 Reach a wooden bench on the right. Next to the bench is an informational sign with a roof. Bear right, still heading generally east. The red-cockaded woodpecker habitat area starts on the left.

0.5 Follow the trail as it jogs left and pass interpretive marker 8. Reach a Y with a wooden bench on the left. Take the right branch and follow the trail until reaching a suspension bridge over the creek. Within 100 yards pass a bench and then reach a Y. Take the right branch, heading west.

0.6 Pass interpretive markers 47, 48, and 49. Cross over a wooden footbridge and bear left and then right at the end of the bridge. The creek is on the right but not visible.

0.7 Pass a wooden bench on the right and across from interpretive markers 52 and 53. Cross a short wooden bridge, with the creek on the right about 7 feet away.

0.8 Cross a short wooden bridge and follow the trail, then within 50 feet cross another wooden bridge. Continue following the trail generally west and cross another bridge. Bear slightly right and pass interpretive markers 57 and 58.

0.9 Continue following the trail as it parallels the creek on the right. Reach a T (this completes the loop) and take the left branch, heading south. The right branch goes to the Flat Car Bridge.

1.0 End the hike at the trailhead.

Jones Forest: Middle Lake Hiking Trail

This hike alternates between trails in the deep woods and dirt park roads. Go by areas set aside for colonies of red-cockaded woodpeckers, an endangered species. Cross a unique land bridge that divides Middle Lake into two parts. This section is interesting because the lake is on both sides of you. The lake is clear and shallow, allowing small fish to be seen from the shore.

Start: Middle Lake Hiking Trail trailhead adjacent to parking area off Gravel Pit Road
Distance: 2.3-mile loop with an out and back
Approximate hiking time: 1.5 hours
Difficulty: Easy due to level terrain
Trail surface: Dirt, sand, gravel
Seasons: Year-round
Other trail users: Bird-watchers, equestrians
Canine compatibility: Leashed dogs permitted
Fees and permits: None required, but must sign in at gate on Gravel Pit Road

Schedule: 8:30 a.m.–5 p.m. Call ahead to see if the trail is open.
Maps: Trail maps available at the park office; USGS: Tamina
Trail contacts: Jones Forest Manager, 1328 FM 1488, Conroe 77384; (936) 273-2261; www .stateparks.com/w_g_jones.html
Other: Restrooms and water are available at the park office. No potable water available on the trails.

Finding the trailhead: From north Houston at the intersection of I-45 and North Sam Houston Parkway East, merge onto I-45 heading north. Follow I-45 North for 19.8 miles to exit 81. Take exit 81 toward FM 1488. Continue for 0.7 mile and take the FM 1488 ramp, going slightly right onto FM 1488. Follow FM 1488 to the park headquarters at 1328 FM 1488. Check in with the ranger and get directions to the Middle Lake Hiking Trail. *DeLorme: Texas Atlas & Gazetteer:* Page 71, F11. GPS: N30 13.787' / W95 29.939'

THE HIKE

Pick up a map at the park office and check with the ranger that the gate at Gravel Pit Road is open. Drive about 1 mile west on FM 1488 to Jones Trail Road. Turn left onto Jones Trail Road and continue a short distance to Gravel Pit Road, which is on the left. Go through the gate to the parking area, fill out a registration card, and deposit it in the collection box. Middle Lake Hiking Trail is one

A grandmother helps her curious granddaughter to identify a shrub leaf while hiking in Jones Forest.

of the few hiking trails in this 1,733-acre forest, as most of the acreage is used as a demonstration and working forest. Use insect repellant to discourage the numerous mosquitoes.

Start at the Middle Lake Trail trailhead adjacent to the south side of the parking area. There is a small lake to the north called North Lake. The hike could be named "wandering around the forest, enjoying the scenery" since there is little signage, except at the park roads. The roads also serve as trails, so using them as reference points helps to keep from becoming disoriented. There are many equestrian trails, but horses are not allowed on this short section. The trail is 7 feet wide and has a sandy dirt surface.

Continue following the trail until reaching a Y. Take the left branch, heading southeast. This is the first of many unsigned trail branches. Not knowing where you're headed adds a touch of adventure. The park foresters use many of these paths as shortcuts to roads or to get to areas to perform their duties. Shade is furnished by the large number of trees, mostly loblolly pines. The average age of the pines is 50 years, so they are mature. Pass by some American beautyberry shrubs, which reach a height of 5 feet. From June through August they have attractive clusters of small bluish flowers. These are followed by small, bright purple berries, appearing from August through November. The berries are a favorite food for wildlife.

Within 0.1 mile reach another Y and keep to the right. Then in a scant 100 yards, come to a Y and take the right branch. Enjoy the sights and sounds of the heavy woods. Watch for a few uprooted trees, remnants of the destruction of Hurricane Ike in 2008. Pass through a clearing and turn right onto the Deep Gully Trail. Equestrians use these trails, so keep to the right and step off the trail for any approaching horses. The woods contains loblolly pines and a mix of hardwoods, including live oaks.

Continue on the Deep Gully Trail. Look for deer tracks and tracks of other animals. Some sections of the forest have been designed as habitat for the endangered red-cockaded woodpecker. These medium-size birds have a rasping *sripp* call. This area allows a good opportunity to see the woodpeckers, especially during spring. Possibly more interesting is to look for nuthatches, which like to buddy around with the red-cockaded woodpecker. They are small, about 4.5 inches long. The easiest way to identify them is by how they climb down tree trunks, headfirst. That's pretty interesting.

Reach the T where the Deep Gully Trail ends at the Middle Lake Trail. Turn right, heading west, and pass the

Middle Lake Picnic Area. There are some yaupon trees here, an invasive species, but their red berries in the fall attract wildlife. Watch for tree roots across the trail. Follow the trail until reaching the western park boundary and turn left. Continue south to the Middle Lake Trail and turn left. Middle Lake is just ahead. This small lake is divided in half by a land bridge. A cluster (group of nesting trees) of red-cockaded woodpeckers is near the lake.

The land bridge is the high point of the hike. Cross over it, with the lake on both sides. Watch for wildlife around the area and a variety of birds. Circle around the south side of the lake, which has a few small cypress trees along the land bridge. This is a great area to kick back and enjoy, with a few picnic tables and excellent shade from the tree canopy. Go west to the park trail and backtrack to the trailhead.

MILES AND DIRECTIONS

0.0 Start at the Middle Lake Trail trailhead adjacent to the south end of the parking area. Head south, going into the forest.

0.1 Reach a Y and take the left branch.

0.2 Follow the trail as the surface turns to grass, until reaching a Y. Take the right branch and follow less than 100 yards to another Y. Take the right branch.

0.4 Continue through a clearing until reaching a park road named Deep Gully Trail. Turn right on Deep Gully. There are road signs at the intersection.

0.6 Pass a maintenance road on the left. Continue following the Deep Gully Trail south, until it ends at the Middle Lake Trail.

0.7 At the T with the Middle Lake Trail, which is a 12-foot-wide road with road signs at the corners, take the right branch, heading west toward Middle Lake.

0.9 Continue on the Middle Lake Trail and pass through a clearing that is the Middle Lake Picnic Area.

1.0 Reach a mowed area with signs identifying it as habitat for a cluster of red-cockaded woodpeckers and bear hard right (north).

1.3 Continue on the path until reaching a T with the Jones Trail. This is the western forest boundary and has a fence. FM 1488 is to the north. Turn left at the T and head south along the fence line.

1.5 Continue following the Jones Trail until the Middle Lake Trail intersects from the left. Turn left onto the Middle Lake Trail, heading east toward Middle Lake.

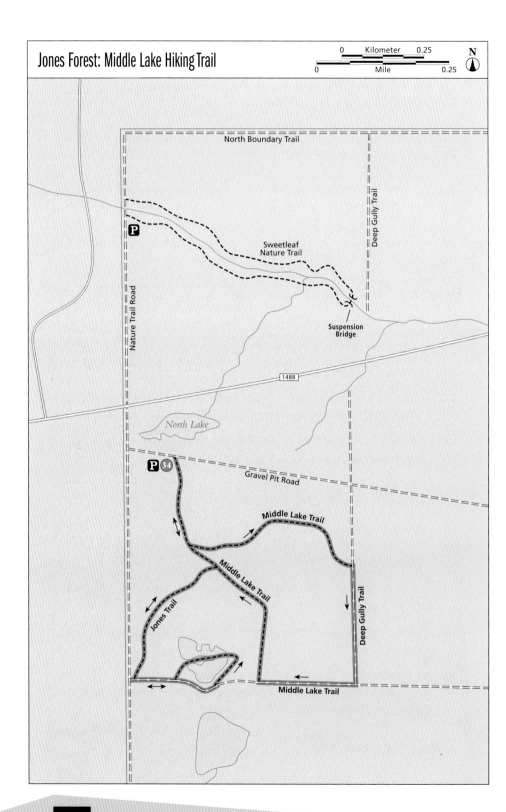

0   Kilometer   0.25

0   Mile   0.25

N

North Boundary Trail

Deep Gully Trail

P

Sweetleaf
Nature Trail

Nature Trail Road

Suspension
Bridge

1488

North Lake

P 34

Gravel Pit Road

Middle Lake Trail

Middle Lake Trail

Jones Trail

Deep Gully Trail

Middle Lake Trail

1.7 Follow the trail, bending to the left, to reach Middle Lake.

1.9 Go around the southern lakeshore to reach the land bridge separating the lake into two parts. Cross over the land bridge and close the loop at Middle Lake Trail. Return to Jones Trail and backtrack to the trailhead.

2.3 End the hike at the trailhead.

A thistle, an attractive but prickly plant, is a noxious invasive species that crowds out native plants.

Houston-Area Hiking Clubs

Houston Happy Hikers
(979) 478-6203
www.houstonhappyhikers.org

Lone Star Hiking Trail Club
113 Ben Dr.
Houston, TX 77022
www.lshtclub.com

Sierra Club Houston Group
P.O. Box 3021
Houston, TX 77253-3021
(713) 895-9309
www.houston.sierraclub.org

The Woodlands Hiking Club
www.woodlandshikingclub.com

Hike Index

Sidebar Index

About the Author

Keith Stelter is a columnist for the HCN newspaper group and has been hiking, writing, and taking photographs for forty years. Growing up, he hiked national park trails with his father, and for the past six years, he has hiked extensively in the Houston and Austin–San Antonio areas. Keith served as executive director of the Texas Outdoor Writers Association in 2006 and 2007 and is a member of the Outdoor Writers Association of America, Texas Master Naturalists, North American Nature Photographers Association, and American Trails Association. He is the author of several books about Texas, including *Best Hikes Near Austin and San Antonio* and Best Easy Day Hike guides for Austin, Houston, and San Antonio. His avocation as a naturalist allows him to add interesting and educational information to his writing. He lives in Tomball, Texas.